THE KEN
COMMANDMENTS

THE KEN COMMANDMENTS

MY SEARCH FOR GOD IN HOLLYWOOD

KEN BAKER

CONVERGENT

NEW YORK

Copyright © 2017 by Ken Baker

All rights reserved.

Published in the United States by Convergent Books, an imprint of the
Crown Publishing Group, a division of Penguin Random House LLC,
New York.

crownpublishing.com

CONVERGENT BOOKS is a registered trademark and the C colophon
is a trademark of Penguin Random House LLC.

Library of Congress Cataloging-in-Publication Data
Names: Baker, Ken, 1970– author.
Title: The Ken commandments / Ken Baker.
Description: First Edition. | New York : Convergent Books, 2017.
Identifiers: LCCN 2017005592 | ISBN 9780451497956 (hc)
Subjects: LCSH: Spiritual biography—United States. | Baker, Ken,
1970– | Celebrities—Religious life—United States.
Classification: LCC BL72 .B34 2017 | DDC 204.092—dc23
LC record available at https://lccn.loc.gov/2017005592

ISBN 978-0-451-49795-6
eISBN 978-0-451-49796-3

Printed in the United States of America

Book design by Chris Welch
Jacket design by Jessie Bright
Jacket photograph by Ramona Rosales
Ornament illustration by Fred Haynes

1 3 5 7 9 10 8 6 4 2

First Edition

For You

CONTENTS

GENESIS

EXODUS

REVELATION

The universe is not outside of you. Look inside yourself; everything that you want, you already are.

—RUMI, SUFI POET (1207–1273)

Religion is like clothing. People want comfort.

—KANYE WEST, AMERICAN HIP-HOP ARTIST (1977–)

GENESIS

In the beginning, God created me.

I went on to live a life of achievements and struggles, joys and pains, successes and failures—both personal and professional.

My journey led me to Hollywood, where I took up a journalism career, at first in magazines, and then television and online, writing and talking about pagan gods and idols known as "celebrities." I would sometimes pray, sometimes attend church, baptized my first child in a Catholic church in Malibu, and considered myself a believer in God.

Over my time in Hollywood, however, I grew distant from my Creator—and from my spiritual self.

It seemed I had it all: a house near the beach, two SUVs, two amazing kids, a marriage filled with a lifetime of amazing memories, a Daytime Emmy Award, book-writing awards, a celebrity journalism career that had sent me around the world covering the richest, most beautiful, talented, and famous humans on the planet. But these were temporary, material, and external rewards, not eternal, spiritual ones. I felt empty.

So after twenty years spent chasing celebrities, writing books, raising kids, and making countless hours of television, I grew plagued with spiritual self-doubt, existential angst, anxiety, and even depression. Indeed, what began as my Hollywood heaven had become my hell. But like Dante wrote in his *Divine Comedy*, I would have to go through hell to get back to heaven.

I decided to use my journalism skills to seek answers to my deepest spiritual questions—including whether God exists and, if so, how I might connect with God before my physical time on Earth ends.

My midlife search for meaning—and for God—took place entirely in Hollywood, the very cradle of celebrity civilization where I had grown so lost.

As a seeker, I chased my spiritual truth just as I had always chased stories as a journalist. Tired of being broken, I was determined to break the biggest news of my life … before I lost my mind. And I soon learned that losing my mind was the very thing I needed to do before I could find myself.

And what I learned, the insights I made and the profound transformation that took place in my life after dedicating myself to assembling the puzzle that was my jumbled soul is herein contained in what shall be known forthwith as …

The Ken Commandments.

THOU SHALL HAVE NO FALSE IDOLS BEFORE THE KARDASHIANS

Some might begin their spiritual journey in a church, sanctuary, temple, or some other traditional house of worship. Others might kick-start their spiritual quest by reading books, going on a retreat with a guru, starting a meditation or yoga practice, or perhaps participating in a Bible study with a rabbi or pastor.

Not me. My search for God begins in Las Vegas while I am keeping up with the Kardashians.

This is not a joke. This really is my life. So how did I get to the point where I am on my knees crying in a hotel room near the Vegas Strip, praying to God for the first time in seemingly forever in an effort to bring a troubled reality star out of a coma?

I'll start my explanation for my peculiar spiritual behavior with a description of what I do for a living: I am the senior correspondent for *E! News* and *E! Online*. While my former professors at Columbia University Graduate School of Journalism might throw up a little in their mouths knowing that

I'm using my degree to report on the frivolity of Hollywood entertainment and celebrity, the truth is that the Kardashian clan is the most important beat I cover. My journalistic identity has become so intertwined with Kris, Kim, Khloe, Kourtney, Kendall, Kylie, Rob, Caitlyn, and the cast of satellite family characters that my *E! News* cohost, Jason Kennedy, has razzed me on the air by calling me Ken Kardashian.

I've been an entertainment journalist for twenty years. It's been a mostly amazing, sometimes maddening (more on that later) career that has taken me from my mid-1990s debut as a wet-behind-the-ears correspondent for *People* magazine, to an *Us Weekly* writer and editor, to a correspondent at *E! News*— the ultimate celebrity-obsessed news organization. Along the way, I've managed to get married, have a son and daughter (and coach both their hockey teams), and succeed (thanks to that anti-tumor medication) in keeping a skull-base pituitary gland tumor I had removed in 1998 from growing back. I also have written many books, one of which was a memoir that was made into the movie *The Late Bloomer*. One of my younger E! coworkers recently observed, "Ken, on paper you have it all."

But paper is easy to shred, burn, or crumple. Only in Hollywood does paper make a soul.

While it may be true that my personal and professional résumé isn't filled with the stuff of crisis, my spiritual résumé tells a much darker story. That document, if I had ever actually spent the time to reflect on the subject long enough to write it, would look more like a maze of meandering lines, dead ends, and blank spaces marking the years that I stopped even pondering my spiritual self, let alone seeking deeper meaning.

A job hazard of doing what I do (really of just leading a

busy, modern life like so many other people do even in places far from the Hollywood sign) has been focusing on others rather than on myself.

Despite all my professional accomplishments and personal adventures, all the incredible life experiences I've racked up, all the people I've met who have influenced my life—highest among them two exceptional children, Jackson and Chloe, and the greatest mom for them in my wife of sixteen years, Brooke—for far too many years my spiritual cup has been evaporating.

My current state is no one's fault but my own. I've chosen to dedicate myself to a strange TV career in which I get paid to gossip about celebrities, live in a hyperactively car-clogged city, and pile on book-writing projects that make me money and give me creative satisfaction but that probably also make my hair fall out.

My life has turned far too frenetic and stressful for me to fully enjoy the beauty and love all around me. In my increasingly scarce "free" time, I have tucked myself away and written book after book (eight in the last sixteen years) in which I tell stories about others, rather than living my own. I need inner rewards, not more book awards. Like many other parents I know, I have chosen to consign my most fundamental health needs and desires to dormancy while I help guide my kids, nurture their budding talents, and create an environment to make their dreams a reality. Empty cup, hollow vessel. Whatever the metaphor, I am it.

My job at *E! News* is to report on the gamut of entertainment news—the most popular TV shows and movies, musicians, as well as the daily hookups, breakups, and screw-ups of the world's biggest stars. The story I've come to cover in Vegas falls firmly into the category of screw-ups. In fact, it involves a celebrity who, after a painfully rapid decline, has just hit rock bottom—mentally, physically, and spiritually.

This latest cautionary tale comes courtesy of former reality star and retired NBA player Lamar Odom, who for the last twenty-four hours has lain in a coma in an intensive care unit a mile from the Vegas Strip.

No media outlet has yet confirmed a detailed explanation for his hospitalization, though there are plenty of rumors—from a suicide attempt to an overdose to an attempted murder at the hands of a prostitute. It's the kind of tabloid-ready mystery that I've come to specialize in solving with the help of my network of in-the-know sources. Fortunately, I've just found out from a coworker that someone I've known for more than ten years is holding vigil at Lamar's bedside.

Since seemingly no one in Hollywood (or seemingly anywhere) actually likes to "talk" on the phone anymore, my calls to her keep going to voice mail. I email her.

Hope you're hanging in there ... What happened???? xo

I drop onto the bed in my hotel room and kill some time scanning emails. A few minutes later, my source who's inside the hospital replies:

Drugs found in his system ... coke and opiates. He was doing crack all weekend. And choked on his mucous.

It's shortly after nine a.m. on a Wednesday in mid-October. I checked into the Vegas Hilton just after midnight, sent here by my bosses back in Los Angeles as soon as word leaked that Lamar had lost consciousness at a brothel.

The thirty-five-year-old former Olympian had fallen into a major funk some three months earlier after his ex, Khloe Kardashian, signed divorce papers. Khloe and Lamar's divorce hadn't been your run-of-the-mill celebrity split. In fact, it was really ugly, even by Hollywood standards. It offered the salacious tabloid spice of Khloe almost instantly beginning to date another handsome pro basketball player—only he was younger, richer and, perhaps most relevant, not a drug abuser.

Lamar's spiral eventually led him to the Love Ranch, a legal brothel in the scrub-brush-scattered desert an hour outside of Vegas, where the 6-foot-10-inch former Lakers forward, who also dabbled in reality TV after he married a Kardashian sister, plunked down $75,000 to spend a few days with two blond prostitutes—one by the professional name of Ryder Cherry and the other Monica Monroe. On Lamar's fourth day of frolicking, which included a liberal intake of "herbal Viagra" pills, a worker found him unconscious in his suite at the bordello and called 911, telling the operator that there was "white stuff coming out of his mouth and blood out of his nose."

The story, as my source reveals to me via email, features the trifecta of tabloid clichés—sex, drugs, and hookers. My years covering celebrity have taught me that the juiciest true Hollywood stories always read far more scandalous than any fiction ever could. Lamar's drama would have been titillating if it weren't all so depressing.

Sleep-deprived and strung out on coffee, I pace the spacious suite, gripping my iPhone as I pepper my source with more questions. The source says she is writing me from the visitor's

lounge outside the ICU. I stand rapt as the information from
her hits my inbox in bits and pieces:

L's condition = "critical"

Unresponsive ... several strokes

posbl brain damage

on ventilator

50-50 chance

My source has asked for her anonymity in exchange for
sharing the facts, to counteract the rumor mill of specula-
tion about what is happening inside that ICU. I know Lamar,
though not nearly as well as my source does. A seemingly
ever-smiling jock I have interviewed many times and social-
ized with at Kardashian family events, Lamar has a reputation in Hollywood as a nice guy who treats everyone—except,
sadly, himself—with respect.

Lamar's self-destructive descent rings familiar to anyone
who follows the travails of celebs even in the most casual way.
Charlie Sheen, Britney Spears, Lindsay Lohan—all had major
issues and somehow they survived. Meanwhile, Whitney
Houston, Michael Jackson, Heath Ledger, Amy Winehouse,
Cory Monteith, and Philip Seymour Hoffman have died. And
this is just a very partial list of celebrity overdoses and/or drug-
fueled meltdowns I have covered in recent years. The list is,
sadly, quite long. After all, infamous overdoses by famous people date back even to well before Marilyn Monroe's in 1962.

Lamar, however, is the current leader in the race to achieving that ignominious distinction.

My friends who follow the Hollywood fame game at a safer, healthier distance often ask me what it is that makes so many celebrities so messed up. I usually give a pat answer like, "Mo' money, mo' problems," or, "Too many options," or "They're insecure narcissists."

Perhaps the difference between me and "them," a profound one when I began working in Hollywood in the mid-1990s fresh from a little newspaper in Virginia, has grown less and less. That is to say, I fear that I have begun falling into some of the same celebrity-like traps I previously witnessed only from the outside looking in.

Enough reflecting and navel gazing, I tell myself. *Back to work.*

I keep emailing with my hospital source.

Still unconscious?

> *yes and no updates. Now having to fix all the damage that was done.*

I quickly write my story on my phone; I want to break the news first, before the TMZs of the world. Less than fifteen minutes after I email it back to the *E! News* room, the exclusive story goes live on *E! Online*: "Drugs Found in Lamar Odom's System; Condition Being Treated as 'Overdose' as Brain Damage 'Likely.'"

E! tweets the post out to its 10 million-plus followers and the story zaps its way through the web, becoming one of the most viewed stories in the history of our website (second only to the 2014 death of my late E! Network colleague Joan Rivers).

As users click, scroll, and share it with friends, I stare out my window at the white concrete Stratosphere Tower punching into the clear blue Nevada sky. The tallest building in Vegas, the Stratosphere is topped by an observation deck nearly nine hundred feet above the ground, from which is perched a bungee-jumping platform. I watch as tourist after tourist jumps off the tower and falls toward the pavement, until they dangle death-defyingly to a bouncy and anticlimactic stop. It doesn't look fun to me. The image reminds me of those haunting ones of people desperately leaping to their death from the flaming windows of the World Trade Center on September 11.

Life is so damn fragile.

The word "love" pops into my mind. Things I've loved: My family, my friends, my job, and my lovers. But do I love myself?

Back to work, really.

Once again, I email my source:

> LMK if there's anything I can do.
>
> *Please pray for Lamar.*
>
> OK, I will.

That's when it hits me like a body crashing to concrete: I can't remember the last time I prayed.

Pray for Lamar.

I am frozen. I want to pray, but I am not sure where to begin, as my thoughts are as mushy as the oatmeal I just ate. I can't pray. Not now. I would be a fraud. I don't want to be one of those people who only talks to God when he needs something. I'm not gonna sit here in Vegas and suddenly dial up God. He'd probably hang up on me anyway.

I'm so tired. The last fifteen hours have passed in a blur.

Earlier that day, watching my eleven-year-old daughter Chloe's ice hockey practice in Long Beach, I got a call from Maureen on the *E! News* desk. Maureen told me to drive straight to Vegas to cover the breaking news—and to call anyone and everyone close to Lamar. Things looked grim. She said to get there fast; Lamar could be dead before I arrived.

Soon, I found myself speeding in my black Mercedes SUV eastward on I-15 toward the California–Nevada line, the moonlight casting shadows on the cacti lining the road. I didn't even have time to pack a bag, let alone reflect on my feelings about someone I knew lying in a coma, or worse.

Now I stand here in silence, but for the meditative hum of the hotel room's air conditioner. A deep question squeezes into the micro-space between my busy thoughts: When will I die?

Sadly, men haven't lived very long in my family. My father, who had type-2 diabetes and heart disease, passed from lung cancer (thanks to cigarettes) at age fifty-one. My uncle Jerry was in his late thirties when he died from heart disease and the effects of diabetes. My father's dad, Grampa Wally, died in his sixties from a heart attack. My older brother, who had just turned fifty-one, suffered heart failure recently and was walking around with a portable defibrillator strapped to his body for over a month.

Experience has taught me life's fragility. Though I didn't exactly need this message hammered into me, three years after my father died in 1998 I underwent cranial base surgery to have a chestnut-size tumor removed from my pituitary gland.

I then wrote a memoir about how having my hormone levels return to normal gave me a second chance in life, which I celebrated two years later by taking leave from magazine writing to live my dream of playing professional hockey.

I had gotten the mortality message: Life is short, we all die, so carpe fucking diem. But the euphoria, zest, gratitude, and momentary spiritual grace I experienced after surviving my health scare had worn off long ago. The peace that I had made with the uncertainty of life, possessing a fearlessness that can come from facing death down, of dancing with the devil and living to tell about it, seems so distant and removed from life today.

In my late twenties and early thirties, I felt blessed for each moment and, as such, did my best to embrace it. I ran marathons for charities, revealed a very personal story about my short-circuited sex life in the book *Man Made: A Memoir of My Body*, approached daily life on a mission to live up to the Jack London quote that filled the very first page of my hockey memoir: "The proper function of man is to live, not to exist. I shall not waste my days in trying to prolong them. I shall use my time."

So how much time do I have left? Do I have a soul that will live on for eternity, as my Catholic teachers taught me at Sunday school? And if so, will my soul reside in heaven or hell? Do I even believe in all that stuff anymore? What the hell do I really believe?

Gosh, I wish I knew. I tell my kids that I believe in God. Seems like the right thing to say, the responsible-parent thing to do. But really, I am clueless. I can't say it with true conviction.

Truth is, I don't know when I will die, nor do I know

what will happen when I do. The uncertainty unnerves me. I wish I knew. I wish I had a faith that answered the questions that I could wrap around me like a Real Housewife's faux fur coat. Alas, I do not. I am naked in the cold of a spiritual netherworld—neither a believer nor a nonbeliever. Just plain lost.

I recently have undergone my annual physical and Dr. Wallace gave me a clean bill of health. But accidents do happen and diseases can come on quickly. After all, life does end on its own schedule—not ours. I realize I'm not delivering any breaking news here, but a fact that haunts me is that death is not an outcome over which we have ultimate control—unless you, say, opt to jump off a tall building with no rope and splatter into countless pieces of bloody flesh, a disturbing image I can't switch off as I look out my window and see more daredevils plunge toward the pavement.

The Vegas Strip, hedonism's Broadway, is a nontraditional place to do such deep, existential thinking. But with a job like mine, I don't easily find myself in quiet, traditional places of sanctuary.

My travel assignments for work tend to happen randomly and require 24/7 focus on the story until my assignment is done. *Whitney Houston's daughter just drowned—go to Atlanta. George Clooney's getting married tomorrow—fly to Italy!* Like a good news soldier, I take on my assignments and wage battle on the front against *Access Hollywood, Entertainment Tonight,* and the ever-growing list of entertainment shows and websites around the world. Besides my smog-filled commutes back and forth to the studio, I am rarely ever by myself. But tonight I am. Rattled by Lamar's fight for his life, however, I suddenly feel as alone as I ever have.

Pray for Lamar.

The voice inside grows louder.

Pray for Lamar.

My heart feels as if it's skipping every other beat. I know what this means. In the last year, I have regularly suffered from what ultimately was diagnosed by a psychiatrist as panic attacks, for which I would be prescribed anti-anxiety pills to use whenever I found myself amid one.

The debilitating episodes began a summer earlier, perhaps not coincidentally, in Vegas. I had just appeared at a bookseller's convention to promote my new novel and was sitting in a middle seat of a Southwest Airlines flight set to return home to Los Angeles. With the temperature on the tarmac pushing 110 degrees, the air inside the cabin was stale, with the AC vent above blowing oven-hot air onto my face. I had been inside stuffy planes many times before, but once we took off the cool air from the higher altitudes would usually breeze into the cabin and all would be good. I hoped this would be the case.

We pushed back from the gate and taxied toward the runway for takeoff. But then the pilot did something unusual. He steered away from the terminal area and rolled us to a desolate patch of pavement on the far edge of the airport. For several minutes that seemed like hours we sat idle in the triple-digit heat. Other passengers began fanning their faces with magazines and fiddling with the air controls in a desperate effort to cool off. Sweat began beading on my forehead and moistening my palms.

Finally, the pilot came on. "Sorry for the delay, folks," he announced calmly (as they *always* do). "Our takeoff has been delayed. Our sensors up here tell us the tires are too hot and we have to wait for them to cool before we can take off. We will update you as soon as we're cleared."

I appreciated the pilot's reassuring report. But still, I sat entombed in an increasingly hotter tube with about a hundred and fifty other people. Five minutes . . . ten minutes . . . twenty minutes . . . half an hour. Still, no update from the pilot. Some passengers began to unclip their seat belts, and one guy stood up and took off his shirt, prompting the flight attendant to bark, "Please remain seated with your belts fastened. We are on an active runway." The grandmotherly lady from Canada seated next to me began to vocalize her inner worry, telling her husband, "We're running out of oxygen!" She turned to me. "What the hell do you think is going on?"

Suddenly, the part of my brain that had compartmentalized my own latent panic collapsed, and my seatmate's fears began to infect me. The jet may have been twelve feet wide, but it seemed like two feet. *You need to get out of this plane!* I unbuttoned the top three buttons on my shirt and fanned the fabric in and out. *OK, calm down, Ken. Just fucking breathe.*

I closed my eyes in an attempt to calm myself with a deep inhale and exhale. But closing my eyes only made it seem like I was locked in a dark box. In fact, my clumsy attempt at meditating (I hadn't even taken a yoga class in a couple of years) made matters worse. I would have, like I did as a kid, prayed to God to bring me peace and ease my worries, but I hadn't done that in years either. I had to face the facts: I had no tools—spiritual, psychological—with which to manage this ordeal. I desperately wanted—needed!—to calm my anxiety-plagued mind. But I couldn't.

Now dizzy and hyperventilating, filled with visions of me twisting open the emergency exit handle and jumping out of the plane to freedom, I unclipped my seat belt and walked quickly toward the front bathroom. Maybe a splash of water on my face would cool me off, I thought. If that didn't work, I didn't rule out a TSA-troubling leap out of the plane via the door.

Just as I approached the bathroom door and the female attendant interrupted me with a "Sir . . ." the pilot came over the PA. "Good news, everyone," he said. "We've been cleared for takeoff."

Relief rolled over me, and I let out all that claustrophobic tension with a long sigh. I turned around and returned to my seat, feeling as exhausted as a marathoner on mile 25. Once midair amid a now-cool cruising altitude, I ordered a glass of Chardonnay to get what is a mere substitute for inner peace, a center, the kind of strength that springs from a spiritual foundation, a faith, a practice, which I was lacking. I had none of those things. I felt isolated, alone. All I had was a glass of wine. I'm so tired of feeling so anxious when I'm alone, I thought.

The day after I landed, I called a psychiatrist. I told him I felt trapped by the life I was living, my real self trapped in a body that seemed to be in a constant state of battle with itself—my mind being the most caustic weapon. He told me the plane was just a symbol. I may have intellectually understood the root of my panic attack, but this understanding wasn't stopping it from happening. I needed pills, I said. A quick fix. I was just trying to survive. And I got some. And I began popping them whenever the Monster awakened. Which had been almost daily.

A year after that, I would suffer my first *on-air* panic attack while hosting my daily morning show *Live from E!* While discussing Donald Trump's latest blunder, I began to black out and had to lean forward onto the glass table rather than fall off my high-backed chair. I came so close to passing out, but somehow didn't. The producers cut away while my co-hosts bantered, allowing me a few moments to unclip my mike and shuffle off the set. I found a couch in the lobby, where I lay down and desperately tried to catch my breath. Luckily, I did.

"Everything OK, Ken?" our show's producer asked me afterward. "You looked white as a ghost."

"Yeah, I'm all right," I lied. "I just didn't eat breakfast."

Now here I am, back in Las Vegas, where I had suffered that first episode on the tarmac—and a similar sense of anxiety is striking me in my hotel room. Not so much the same "trapped" feeling of that plane, and not the near-blackout of my on-set episode, but rather feeling untethered and anchorless and not having a solid sense of my spiritual self, of feeling lost in the world. What is the point of this all? I wondered.

As a psychotherapist years ago had instructed me to do in such moments, I close my eyes, suck in the dry Nevada air, and breathe in deep and let it out. It doesn't work. But rather than popping a Xanax, I begin doing something a pill-prescribing doctor has never once recommended: I drop to the floor on my knees and talk to a friend I haven't communicated with in a very, very long time:

God, thank you for bringing me here safely today. Please watch over Lamar, please help him find the strength to live and give strength to his friends and family. Amen.

I open my eyes. I don't believe my prayer will make a difference in whether Lamar Odom will ever wake from his coma. I mean, doesn't God have more important things to worry about than a coked-out former NBA player? There's the Islamic State, millions dying from cancer, poverty, war, pestilence. But then again, I don't *not* believe in the possibility of divine intervention. OK, honestly, I have no fucking idea what I believe anymore, and I sorely miss the days when I did.

I turn away from the floor-to-ceiling window and flop onto the couch. I sink in and, with my hands folded in prayer, tears tumble down my cheeks like dice on a craps table. After a restless night of semi-sleep, I had thought my eyes were too dry and crusty to cry. But like I'd been doing with a lot of things in my life, I thought wrong.

II

LISTEN TO THY SELF . . .
AND
WHITNEY HOUSTON

I get up from the hotel couch and walk over to my ninth-floor window, staring out at nothing and everything at the same time. The blurry space I see might as well be my soul. But I've had enough with all this black and white. It's time to fill in the drab canvas with the color of spirit. At forty-six, I am finally going to get serious about finding God. I vow to dedicate the better part of the next year to stop using the Celebrity Industrial Complex as my excuse for why I am not focused on spiritual matters and, instead, use Hollywood as a laboratory to figure out what I believe, to define exactly what my relationship with God is . . . and to determine whether I even believe He/She/It exists.

The list of things *not* missing in my life—a supportive family, decent health, some financial security—is long, yet the void I was feeling stemmed from not having the one thing I had lost touch with over my years in Hollywood: God.

And I don't just mean the biblical, paternalistic God—that fire-and-brimstone, Ten Commandments–declaring omniscience of

my Catholic childhood who demanded that you accept Jesus
Christ as your savior and commit no sins or else . . . you go to
hell! What I miss is having a faith in any Higher Power. I mean,
I have friends who are addicts who, as part of their twelve-step
program, believe in one. Yet, apparently, I don't have what even
recovering crackheads do: Faith. I want to believe in something
that might elevate me above the spiritual superficiality of work
and drive-by parenting that fills me with a near-constant guilt
that I am failing my family by traveling so much and being oc-
cupied by yesterday, tomorrow—and not the moment.

I come home night in, night out to be with my family,
but I am too often not "there" with them. Instead, I am distracted by my emails or lost in outlining my next book or so
consumed with anxiety over anything stressful that I, more
often than not, come home and camp out in the bedroom, lose
myself in my laptop, or veg out on the couch watching NHL
game highlights. I feel so damn lost. And if I continue to float
on my raft down this isolation river, I fear—actually, no, I
am convinced—that all of this is not going to end well. I too
could become a Hollywood cliché. I don't think I am being
melodramatic when I say that I could be Lamar.

But that's getting ahead of myself—something I am very
good at, by the way. Projecting myself into the future and all
its uncertainty, and in so doing making my present as uncomfortable as a priest watching a Seth Rogen sex comedy in front
of his congregation.

I don't have spiritual peace, a calming center that might
come from having a firmer sense of what will happen when
I meet my maker. I don't need all the answers; I just want to
dive into something far deeper than the spiritual kiddie pool
in which I find myself splashing.

After twenty years in Hollywood interviewing the rich and famous (and by becoming a TV personality blurring the lines between me and them), I have in far too many ways, if not entirely, become the kind of materialistic, spiritually superficial person I never set out to be.

OK, fine. Maybe I'm being too hard on myself. I have a history of being my own worst critic, a holdover of my competitive hockey-playing days where I was trained to believe that no matter what you achieve, "you're only as good as your last game." As a result, I critique nearly everything—my on-air performance, my book prose, my parenting, my gym workout. There's virtually no activity that I engage in that isn't followed by some sort of I-could've-done-that-better analysis. At various points in my career I've tried to lay off the critical gas and mute this negative inner monologue, only to return to it, as it's the only driving style that has kept my career barreling down the Hollywood highway. But what good is such a security blanket if it ends up suffocating you?

To be fair to myself, I haven't totally "gone Hollywood" and descended into self-loathing, self-obsessed, narcissistic madness. My primary focus in my life for the last ten years has been on providing and caring for my family, trying to be a decent person at work and at home, in general just trying to follow the Golden Rule. I want to be a good role model to my kids and do so by working hard, rushing home from the TV studio after work whenever possible for the kids' ice-hockey practice and giving them, from the perspective of someone who himself played college and pro hockey back in the day, words of wisdom on a regular basis. Six years ago, I even helped a friend, Olympic skater and born-again Christian Scott Hamilton, write a self-improvement book on how to be happy in the face of adversity and everyday obstacles. But somewhere along the way I have failed to practice what we preached in that book. I wonder, Am I a fraud?

I've come to spend far more time doing things like getting makeup smeared on my face every day for the lights and cameras, listening to Howard Stern on the car radio during hour-long freeway commutes, watching NHL games on the tube and scheduling regular teeth-whitening appointments instead of meditating, praying, or engaging in any activities aimed at deepening my spiritual self.

I haven't been nourishing my soul like I did before I became consumed with things that used to matter to me but now seem so vapid: Being a familiar face to millions on TV in over 150 countries, amassing several hundred thousand social media followers and fans. Maybe it is mid-career burnout. It messes with your mind knowing on a daily basis your face and voice and body is being zapped in the form of electrons into the eyes of total strangers, and you don't know them or see them or have any way to interact with them. Perhaps to some this seems like a healthy energy transfer, and it is a karmic blessing that I can connect with so many people. But I feel as though this media-enabled energy transfer is predominantly one-sided, leaving me with some sort of a deficit. This, of course, is a very wonky way to describe a very simple dynamic: I am giving away a lot, but not getting a lot back in return. The math doesn't compute well for my concept of what makes a nourished soul.

This at least partially explains the persistent anxiety, the occasional panic attacks, and the overall existential emptiness of the kind that grips me in my Vegas hotel room.

And now, after years of soul neglect, I am ready to make a conscious choice to press Pause on this movie that is my life.

The stakes are high. My mind is frazzled, my body aches, my stomach refuses to digest much of anything without rejecting it with moans and groans. My innards can't handle dairy, spices, fried foods, red meat—basically anything that requires a strong, healthy body to metabolize it. Worse, except for when the cameras are on, I am not smiling very often anymore. Something is rotting from the inside out. Maybe a preacher would call it Satan. A shrink would call it anxiety. I call it no way to live.

If I don't embark on a soul-searching mission to find my spiritual truth, if I don't answer this call from what I can only decipher as the Voice of God, I'm afraid I won't make it much longer. I fear I am not even living; I am dying.

If I walked into an Alcoholics Anonymous meeting right now, they might wonder why I showed up. For starters, I don't drink alcohol. Other than popping the occasional panic-attack-combating Xanax, I also don't abuse drugs. Yet there is no doubt that I would fit right in at a support-group meeting.

As unhealthy as it is for my overall health, I crave tension, uneasiness, pressure, insecurity; it is my good luck charm that I have learned to carry in order to achieve my goals. *Never get too comfortable. You're only as good as your last game.*

For so many of my years, I have been fueled by a high that comes from walking life's tightrope without a net—in secular pursuits with little sign of mindfulness, clarity, peace, or grace, which are the very qualities that I want to possess. Instead, I ride a wave of adrenaline and egoistic performance thrill that by the end of each day leaves my nerves so frayed I am afraid to close my eyes because the person I meet in that quiet silence is really not one with whom I want to spend time alone. How ironic that worshiping my ego so much has left me being completely not at peace with myself.

So what would happen if (despite my not remembering the last time I got tipsy, let alone drunk) I walked into an AA meeting? I know exactly what I would do: I would sit down in the circle and announce, "My name is Ken and I am a Self-Aholic." Then I would take my cue from page one of the AA playbook and declare, "I am powerless over my addiction—and as a result my life has become spiritually unmanageable."

But I have worked for twenty years in Hollywood—the capital of Secular Self-Worship—yet I have never heard of Self-Aholics Anonymous. Why? Because it doesn't exist! When it comes to submitting to and bowing before a force greater, wiser, more insightful than yourself, there is no one place where people like me who are suffering can go and get fixed in any step-by-step way. While there isn't one go-to God place, there is no shortage of places to go within the "Thirty Mile Zone" of Hollywood, as TMZ terms it. Each day, as I hustle about my business of attending events, interviewing celebrities, hosting shows, I pass by churches, mosques, synagogues, Scientology centers, meditation studios, Buddhist temples, and various nondenominational spiritual places of worship. Inside these places, I am told, are gifted pastors, gurus, yogis, masters, and teachers, all of whom are helping suffering souls to get in touch with a spiritual realm, connect with a Higher Power, worship an entity other than the Self.

Now that I have prayed for Lamar, I remember how easy it is to pray. You just close your eyes and talk (silently, unless you want people to think you are a loony toon). Back when I was a competitive hockey player, I would pray often. Don't worry. I wasn't one of those annoying jocks who thinks God gives two craps about whether they win a silly game. It's so off-putting when some jughead scores a touchdown and immediately points to heaven. Seriously, c'mon! If you're going to praise Him for a touchdown, you should also point to heaven when you blow the game with a stupid mistake. After all, I was taught in Sunday school that God gives us lessons through positive and negative experiences. So, no, I wasn't one of those self-glorifying jocks. Instead, I would pray for protection and thank God for allowing me to play the sport I love. I found that it settled me, made me feel like there was less pressure on myself knowing I had a relationship with a greater power who didn't care about the outcome of my match. Therefore, it only makes logical sense that if prayer helped me be better on the ice, then it should help me better off the ice in "real" life. Sure, there's as much sports psychology involved in this as spiritual psychology, but, hey, if it centers you it centers you.

When I played hockey back in college at Colgate University, I kept the Serenity Prayer taped to my locker-room stall:

God, grant me the serenity to accept the things I cannot change,
Courage to change the things I can,
And wisdom to know the difference.

I didn't know it at the time, but the Serenity Prayer, written by the late American theologian Reinhold Niebuhr, is a staple at Alcoholics Anonymous meetings.

Which brings me back to me being the charter member of "Self-Aholics Anonymous," which of course doesn't exist. And since there is no one place for one to go discover God as one goes to AA to attain sobriety, I will embark on a self-directed journey.

But for now, I will go back to fantasizing about what would happen if I joined AA. After I embraced the first of the recovery program's twelve steps, I would vow to take Step Two: *That I have come to believe a Power greater than myself can restore me to sanity.*

Or so I hope. But the only way to know if I can find "God" will be to go and try to climb my personal stairway to heaven. Step by step. And in either a cheesy coincidence or a sign from God, as I am somewhere between Barstow and the Nevada state line driving back to L.A. from Lamar's near-death coma in Vegas, I spin through the satellite radio channels, and Whitney Houston is singing . . .

I'm gonna take it slowly 'cause I'm making it mine
Step by step . . .

III

STUDY THE BOOK OF HOWARD STERN

I've long been the type of person who has to think through something, dissect it, fully understand it, overanalyze it to the point of near mental exhaustion, before I can move ahead and take action. In other words, I am a lot like most people: I think way too much, about too many things, way too often.

As a result, when it comes to deciding whether to take on a new project, buy something, write a book, make friends, I don't just jump in without analyzing the logic of a decision— weighing pluses and minuses, the relative merit of my choice. Ultimately, I always ask myself: Will the investment of my time and energy yield a result that will make the effort worthwhile?

So it's entirely consistent with my character that I haven't even quite started my journey to find God in Hollywood and I'm already making it an exercise in egoistic overthinking.

The reason for my trepidation isn't because I don't want to find God. In fact, I deeply desire making the discovery—or rediscovery—of that connection. In the past, at times when I had faith in a greater, wiser force in the universe with whom I could talk, thank, ask for guidance, I was a happier, healthier, more content and productive human being. So it's a no-brainer for me to want to find that kind of sacred space again.

· Even so, there's a red light preventing me from stepping on the gas pedal that might lead me back to God. And like most things in my life that have gnawed at me, what hinders me now is a question: Does God even exist? After all, atheism, the belief that deities do not exist, is at least as old as theism itself.

I've experienced what I have interpreted as seeing "God" at various moments in my life—in a sunset over the horizon on the island of Kauai, praying in times of crisis, emerging from brain surgery with a new lease on life, looking into the eyes of my newborn children, moments of stillness hiking in the mountains or splayed out on a yoga mat, making love with someone for the first time, drenched in sweat on the ice amid a hockey game in which I felt like I had transcended my physical self. But I still can't prove beyond a reasonable doubt to anyone, no less myself, that God exists. In fact, no one can. Not the pope, not the Dalai Lama; no highly enlightened mortal has yet come up with the irrefutable "evidence" of the type that the Western ego-mind has come to demand as proof of anything these days. That's why they call it *believing* in God, not *knowing* there's a God. It requires belief—a leap of faith.

On the other hand, it would also take a leap for me to conclude I do not believe even in the slightest possibility of a Higher Power behind all that we experience as the universe.

The more I think about this question—that the very premise of my search for God may be faulty—it seems reasonable for me to poke the anti-faith bear before I go chasing something that may be a fantasy, a psychological crutch, a comforting myth that we humans have concocted and codified to make the bleak reality of our inevitable demise less damn depressing and mysterious.

Luckily, finding atheists in Hollywood is about as easy as finding injected lips and fake boobs—that is, they are seemingly everywhere you look. But some (atheists, not implants) are more vocal and articulate about their anti-faith faith than others.

I remember hearing Howard Stern being asked if he believed in God, to which he replied, "I know intellectually there is no God. But in case there is, I don't want to piss Him off by saying it."

Not only is Howard's candor good comedy, it's also poignant. While I *think* in my heart that I believe in God, I don't *know* this to be true in my brain with any certainty. So if and when I get to the mythical pearly gates, it makes sense to hedge my bets in favor of there being a God, just in case. That is, it seems more plausible than implausible. Certainly, I would profess faith in the biblical God before I would in Kanye "Yeezus" West being the Messiah. I have met many of these kind of wishy-washy, better-safe-than-sorry believers in my life. I call them the Just-in-Case Christians. As in, they're gonna go through the motions of believing . . . just in case. Call it the Gospel According to Howard Stern.

But so often throughout history religious folks have made it so hard to buy into their dogmas. Comedian and liberal political commentator Bill Maher has made rants against organized religion a staple of his routine. Maher even made a documentary about how ridiculous religion is (aptly titled *Religulous*).

Maher, like many in the modern, post–Scientific Revolution atheist camp, shuns any belief system that is not "evidence-based." But he also has said, "I am open to anything for which there is evidence. Show me a God and I will believe in Him," at the same time defining faith as "the purposeful suspension of critical thinking."

While there are plenty of pro-faith celebrities promoting various religious traditions, the list of those who have declared their lack of faith in God is long, among them Emma Thompson, Billy Joel, Jodie Foster, Julianne Moore, Daniel Radcliffe, Keira Knightley, James Cameron, Seth MacFarlane, Ricky Gervais . . . and it goes on and on.

But included on that list is someone I know: Adam Carolla. Adam is a comedian, mega-popular podcaster, radio host, and author whom I met many years ago when I was a correspondent for *People*.

Along with his pal Jimmy Kimmel, the often acid-tongued Adam served as co-host of a short-lived but memorably absurd variety show on Comedy Central called *The Man Show*, in which the two dudes sat at a bar and celebrated the macho clichés of modern manhood: beer, sports, chicks, beer. Every episode ended with "Cheerleaders Jumping on Trampolines," a segment in which, well . . . the title speaks for itself.

A middle-aged man obsessed with cheerleaders may seem an unlikely interview subject with whom I would choose to address the deepest of deep questions: whether God exists. But I've been around Adam long enough to know that, really, he's a button-down thinker wrapped in a mechanic's jumpsuit.

Adam and I have run into each other over the years—on a radio show he used to host, at a celebrity grand prix or two, one time at a furniture store on La Brea Avenue in Hollywood— and we have some mutual friends. I wouldn't call us best friends by any stretch of the definition, but I do have his number (which often qualifies one as a bona fide friend among the Hollywood set).

Adam has long been a vocal atheist, voicing very impassioned explanations for his opinion on the topic of God, religion, and faith, including this definitive declaration on his radio show:

> I am not agnostic. I am an atheist. I don't think there's no God. I know there's no God. I know there's no God the way I know many other laws in our universe. I know there's no God and I know that most of the world knows that as well. They just won't admit it because there's another thing they know: they are going to die. And it freaks them out. Most people don't have the courage to admit that there's no God and that they know it. . . . It freaks them out. Because life is filled with tragedy and it's filled with worse than tragedy: the unknown.

I sent Adam an email a few weeks ago telling him about my "search for God," and about how I had decided to write a book about it since there are a lot of other people out there also trying to figure out what the heck they believe and hey, maybe reading about my journey will in some way help them figure out what they believe. Or what they don't believe. Which is where Adam comes in.

I suggested we meet up at a church or synagogue or some other counterintuitively clever place to talk about this topic. But we couldn't find a time that matched our busy schedules, so Adam, as known for being a car nut as he is for being opinionated, suggested he call me while he is in his preferred place of worship: his car.

It's a Saturday morning and I can hear in the background the rumble of the road as he's driving on Highway 14 to a racing school in the desert an hour north of L.A.

"Ken, I gotta be honest with ya," Adam says in his trademark nasal twang that always makes him sound cranky. "Growing up, I never set foot inside a church. In fact, I never spent any time around religious people until I was probably twenty-four and worked installing closets with some born-again Christian gang-bangers who had found religion in jail."

"That was really your first exposure?" I ask. "You had never even been dragged to church?"

"Well, yeah," Adam says. "I mean, I had seen weirdo preachers on TV and would see people going in and out of church or whatever, but I just didn't grow up with religion. It wasn't something my family ever talked about and so I never really thought about it. I grew up in a weird spiritual vacuum in North Hollywood in the '70s. My family wasn't atheists, per se. Religion was just not something we ever discussed. So I have never had a leaning toward [it] and I have never felt the need to search for anything."

I tell him I was raised Roman Catholic, attended Sunday school, and that I was taught you could talk to God through prayer, which He may or may not answer, but that He heard. "It always made me feel good knowing God was there," I explain. "Sort of like having a friend with you all the time who will listen."

"I respect that, Ken," Adam says. "I'm not saying you're an idiot for talking to a God you have never seen or heard or can even prove exists. I'm not one of those atheist guys who think that. I'm just saying that, to me, maybe simply because, unlike you, it wasn't something I was taught, I think it's all fantasy. No offense to you, if you still think that God will—"

"Honestly, I'm not sure what I think anymore," I butt in. "That's why I wanted to talk to you. I think you could be right. Maybe there is no God. Maybe I will be better off—and happier—if I stop stressing out over finding something that doesn't exist."

Adam laughs. "Hey, man. Don't get me wrong. I think the world would be a better place if everyone followed the Ten Commandments starting tomorrow and thought that talking to God rather than blowing shit up and hurting people was a better choice in life. But you don't need religion to be a good person. You don't need some dude in a beard and stone tablets to claim God gave him those. Religious people make the argument quite often that God determines right from wrong, but I find that line of thinking a little bit insulting. Intuitively, I believe nature has an order to it and it has instilled that moral compass in our brains. Think about it, Ken. We are not programmed to eat our kids upon birth because that wouldn't work well from a natural, evolution standpoint. There would be, like, zero natural order in it. I didn't eat my kids when they were born because it is not my instinct—not from my fear of God or that the LAPD will arrest me. Another example is that it is not in me to kill someone or steal possessions. These are all things we rely on not only for us in nature, but also our species and other species as well. You don't need to be religious to know right from wrong. I don't need a sanctioning body to tell me that it is wrong for me to stand behind you in line at Pinkberry and take your vanilla sundae out of your hand. It's just obvious. What's yours is yours and mine is mine. That is how we both can coexist. It's best for our species. It's something that is wired into our DNA so that we can propagate our species."

Clearly, I have reached out to the right atheist.

"Can I chime in for a second?" I interrupt his rant.

"Of course," Adam says. "Sorry, I just don't shut up when it comes to this topic."

I tell Adam that Bill Maher likens believing in God to believing in Santa Claus.

"Would you agree with Bill? I ask him.

"Well, I am pretty darn close to Bill Maher on that topic," Adam says. "I think we all can agree that Santa Claus doesn't exist, OK. But even though he doesn't exist, I can tell you that he has brought a lot of joy to my kids. Not only do they love the idea of Santa Claus, but also his little Elf on the Shelf, which by the way is another magical godlike deity. I have no problem with them believing in Santa as long as they aren't hurting themselves or others. That's the problem with religion. The whole religion-on-religion crime thing is out of control and has been for thousands of years. Look at what is happening in the Middle East on a daily basis. I don't like religions in the sense that often it creates two teams. At some point, one team always decides that the other team needs to be eliminated. I like Judaism, but I don't like [how] they're always fighting with Muslims and vice versa. I don't like that division. It creates a battle that has shed a lot of blood over the years. There are many religions that are peaceful. If everyone were just a Buddhist I wouldn't give a shit. There are many religions that are peaceful and I don't mind those at all. Religion just seems like an outdated thing. I don't think we need it anymore. It causes more harm than good."

While not exactly a theologian, Adam is making some sense. Much of what he is saying is stuff I have thought myself at some point, logical conclusions based on observing what crazy things people do in the name of God. But while I do agree with Adam that organized religion has divided as much—or more than—as it has united, the question of God's existence is, to me, a whole other department outside of religion. In fact, I feel as if my faith in a God, however slight, might come from an instinctual, almost cosmic connection to the universe.

I have never been able to commit to an anti-God belief anywhere near as much as Adam. There's an argument that I can't be anti-God because I was brainwashed at an early age to believe. Fair enough. But my inability to *not* see the hand of God in our material life extended well beyond my easily impressionable childhood, and into college, when I could make adult, sensible observations.

Case in point: As an undergrad at Colgate University, I majored in geology, and something that always led me back to believing in a God or a force or a Higher Power or a Great Architect was that whether I was studying the molecular structure of a quartz crystal or a slab of volcanic rock, it all seemed so perfectly complex that my critical mind kept concluding it couldn't have been created randomly.

And even if it were created by total luck and happenstance, who or what created and enabled that randomness to happen? I have never found any definitive answer to this question. To me it seems more likely than not that a force of some sort is behind it all.

"But who or what made our DNA?" I ask Adam. "What programmed our genetic computers not to kill each other?"

Adam sighs. "Look, the honest answer is that I don't fucking know. But that doesn't mean I have to go believing in something just in case God made all this shit—you know, just to hedge my bets."

"But don't you wonder how this reality we experience came into existence?" I ask. "I mean, I do. All the time. Not knowing what or who made all this really bugs me."

"Of course I have thought about that!" he answers, sounding rather indignant. "But maybe the difference between you and me is that I am OK with not knowing. Reality is something you should only look for when you are really high, my friend. If you're not rolling on peyote, then reality is this: The sun comes up, you wake up and go about your day and then the sun goes down. I am driving a car right now and if I mash the pedal down I will smash into this Hyundai in front of me. That is reality. Why do I need to come up with an answer to what made all this stuff I am experiencing as my reality? I have a lot of questions I don't have an answer to—like why am I not attracted to dudes? I don't know, I'm just not. That's good enough for me."

"Well," I say, "I've tried not to care or not to need to know, but I can't. I feel like I have this brain asking questions and it would be lazy of me, kind of irresponsible, not to examine it and try to answer them. I mean, that is what a lot of religion is about. It's a framework, a set of stories and beliefs that help explain it all. I'm not saying they're right or wrong, but I respect the intention because I also want to know. I want answers."

"Ken, I am totally open to there being an answer that proves there is a God. If someone came up with a good argument, some solid evidence that there is a God or whatever, I would accept it. I would love nothing more than a good argument to get me talked out of being an atheist. It would take a lot of the mystery out of the world and I bet that would make a lot of people feel a whole lot better about life. But humans have been trying to make various arguments for why God exists for thousands of years and they still haven't nailed it."

As Adam pontificates, I realize I am pinching my brow and getting frustrated. Not because I necessarily disagree with Adam's take on this God business, but because the more I listen to him the more I feel like I have left the state of California and entered the state of confusion.

"OK, OK," I interrupt. "Can I ask you something?"

"You just did."

I ignore his joke and turn serious. "The more I listen to you, the more I just want to know your bottom-line answer to this question: Do you think there is any chance that God exists?"

I can still hear the hum of his tires on the road. But I don't hear Adam.

I break the silence. "In other words," I say, "would you bet your life on it?"

"Uhhhhhmmmmhuuuuh." Adam is making a sound somewhere between pondering and moaning. "That's a real good question," he says. "Look, if I told you that there is a zero percent chance of there being a God, I would be as guilty of being a hypocrite as much as some religious nut who believes I am going to hell because I don't worship their God."

"Wait a second," I say. "You sound more like Carl Sagan than Bill Maher."

"The astronomer guy?" Adam asks.

"Yeah."

"What did Sagan say about all this God stuff?"

Luckily, I know the answer. Before talking to Adam, I had

done a little research on the subject of atheism, and a lot of articles popped up on the late scientist's take on the possibility of a God. Sagan, perhaps best known for his research into extraterrestrial life, was one of the first scientists who popularized the field of cosmology through his work in books and on TV, most famously as host of the PBS series *Cosmos*.

"Well, people assumed he was an atheist, but he wasn't," I explain. "He actually considered himself agnostic."

I find a couple Sagan quotes on my laptop and read them aloud to Adam:

> I am not an atheist. An atheist is someone who has compelling evidence that there is no Judeo-Christian-Islamic God. I am not that wise, but neither do I consider there to be anything approaching adequate evidence for such a god. Why are you in such a hurry to make up your mind? Why not simply wait until there is compelling evidence?

> An atheist has to know a lot more than I know. An atheist is someone who knows there is no God.

I add, "The gist of it is that Sagan didn't believe in a God, but he was very open to the idea. He just hadn't seen enough evidence to support what he called the 'God Hypothesis,' saying, 'I'd be fully willing to accept if there were compelling evidence; unfortunately, there is nothing approaching compelling evidence.'"

"So, there ya go!" Adam says brightly. "I would say I am with Sagan on this topic. I am probably about one percent agnostic. The rest of me is an atheist."

"So then, you think God might actually exist?"

"Yeah," he says. "But I am ninety-nine percent sure there is nothing."

"So then, you realize that you're not actually an atheist?"

"By that definition, no."

"But you're all over YouTube as one of the biggest atheists in Hollywood." I laugh. "Did I just break some news here?"

"Yeah, but not really," Adam jokes. "I'm still putting my money on there being no God."

Adam says he's gotta go, explaining that he is late for his hot-rod racing session at the track. So I thank him and we hang up. And as Adam is about to drive in circles at high speed, my brain revs in its own circles as I process that I had just interviewed one of the supposedly most ardent atheists in Hollywood but ended up basically converting him into an agnostic. This was not at all my intention. My plan was to be open to possibly being persuaded by Adam that the "God Hypothesis" is a flawed one not worth spending years trying to gather evidence for, not worth being wracked with existential angst over to the point where I am having panic attacks. Instead, I've come away from it feeling like some sort of proselytizer for theism, or, at the very least agnosticism.

I leave my house and go for a walk down to the ocean to watch some beach volleyball, hoping to take my mind off all this deep-shit debate. Despite my best effort to zone out under the sun, I can't stop thinking about Adam's philosophical flip-flop.

So I call my oldest brother, Kevin. Six years older than me, Kevin has long been my go-to for all things spirituality. Kevin, who lives outside Buffalo, New York, majored in Bible studies and for nearly twenty years pastored a nondenominational

Christian church. Whenever I have a question about religion, I tap his vast knowledge. He is sort of my God Google.

"What's up, brother?" Kevin answers.

I cut right to the chase. "I was wondering what the Bible says about atheists."

Kevin scans his biblical brain for a few moments before replying, "Well, Christians often start with Psalm 14. Check that out."

Thanks to my ear buds, I am hands-free and can search the passage on my phone and read it aloud to him.

Only fools say in their hearts,
"There is no God."
They are corrupt, and their actions are evil;
not one of them does good!

"That's pretty cut and dried," I conclude. "The God in the Bible leaves no room for doubt."

Kevin laughs. "Not exactly. I mean, God recognizes that humans will have doubt. It is part of the human experience. But why do you ask?"

I tell him about my conversation with Adam Carolla, how he basically waffled on his longstanding atheism position, and how in the process I realized that I am definitely not an atheist. "But I do have my doubts," I add.

"That's OK," my brother says. "That means you are seeking. You should treat this search, this spiritual investigation that you're doing, like one of your journalism projects. Ask the hard questions. God will lead you to the truth."

IV

PRAY WITH
GWEN STEFANI

My relationship with the Bible has been as on again/off
again as the relationships of some of the tumultuous celebrity couples I cover in my job. In fact, I have probably broken up more times with the Bible than Justin Bieber did with
Selena Gomez.

As a kid, I did the Sunday school thing, learned the Ten
Commandments and acquired a basic knowledge of scripture—or at least enough to know that the Old Testament is
all the stuff before Jesus came on the scene. All right, maybe
I learned more than that. But barely. I wasn't much of a
reader—or a listener.

And then, as I entered young adulthood I began to cast
major doubt on the truth of all the stories, considering doozies
like the world being created in six days and God needing to
rest for only one day after manifesting all that infinite mass.
Then, in college, I took a few religion classes and studied the
Bible from a more academic perspective, which left me with
a greater appreciation for the Bible as a guide to life, if not a

totally accurate historical document. But in my mid-twenties and thirties, my religion became my journalism, in which I sought "truth" through my work and pretty much stayed away from the Bible and organized religion. It helped that I married a woman who had zero interest in organized religion.

I did, however, read a lot of books about Buddhism and spiritual self-improvement, including *The Power of Now* by Eckhart Tolle and the *Seven Laws of Spiritual Success* by Deepak Chopra. At that time, the Bible seemed less and less relevant, more of an archaic text and collection of allegorical stories than something real and true that connected with modern-day life.

But I have always had respect for Christians who believe and follow the teachings of the Bible, especially preachers who are earnest in their faith and their commitment to spreading the Word . . . as long as they don't hate, shun, and judge those who don't.

In Hollywood, which has a reputation for being as culturally secular (and, more often, hedonistic) as any major industry on the planet outside of pornography, there is actually an underground army of faithful Christians who have, in the last decade or so I have noticed, become more visible.

I have seen their rise personally through my fellow *E! News* host Jason Kennedy, who had been inviting me for years to come to his weekly Bible study in Beverly Hills. I never accepted his gracious invitations, but a year ago I did RSVP yes to his wedding in Dallas, Texas, to his fiancée, Lauren.

Both evangelical Christians, their Bible-based ceremony reflected their faith. The minister liberally populated his sermon with frequent references to Jesus, and many more to the Bible and, of course, plenty of Amens.

In media interviews leading up to the wedding, Jason and

Lauren credited God for bringing them together. But as a not-so-sure believer, I left open at least the possibility that the news media was more responsible for their coupling than the Creator and a two-thousand-year-old religious tradition. But maybe that was me being cynical. After all, cynicism is the armor we don in order not to feel life.

In 2011, Lauren, a fashion blogger and model, suffered a horrific accident with a plane propeller that had cost her an eye and her left arm, a tragic story that had received national media attention, including from Jason, who along with hordes of other journalists, tracked the drama of her fight back to health. The nation followed her road to recovery like a fairy tale that ended with her getting a prince in the form of Jason.

My private doubts about divine providence aside, their wedding in an ornate suburban Dallas hotel ballroom, filmed for an E! Network special, *Lauren and Jason Get Married*, was heartwarming, spiritually enriching, and romantic. I cried.

At the reception, I stood alone sipping a glass of white wine when a man approached me. Thin with pale skin, he wore black-frame glasses that made him look the stereotype of a Silicon Valley nerd or video-game geek.

"I'm Judah." He reached for my hand and shook it with enthusiasm, a wide smile, and popping eyes. "I'm a big fan. Watch ya all the time on E!"

"Well, I know who you are too," I replied.

Suddenly, I recognized him.

We had never met, but I had heard and read a lot about pastor Judah Smith, a friend of Jason's who had been hosting the aforementioned weekly Bible study in Beverly Hills that was in vogue for many young Hollywood stars. With a youthful demeanor and straight-talking sermonizing that didn't come across as "preachy," Judah had been serving as a spiritual mentor to celebrities such as Justin Bieber, Gwen Stefani, and Selena Gomez. In so doing, the energetic preacher had become something of a celebrity himself, known for tailoring his sermons to the celebrity set. He tweaked his message to address head-on the pressures of fame, materialism, sex, and the overall temptations that come with the territory. And this Bible study, I was told by Jason, was a safe zone for celebrities, with Judah often reminding attendees that everyone in the room is to be treated with respect, not like some sort of zoo animal to be gawked at or hounded for selfies.

"It's not easy to be a man of faith," Judah once said in an interview. "There's a lot of options in modern culture and modern society, particularly when things are afforded to you on a celebrity status."

Judah had just turned thirty-five but looked at least ten years younger, and as we chatted at the wedding reception I found his folksy charm disarming. I realized why so many stars would be attracted to him. After a few minutes of conversation, I could see that Judah possessed an innate talent to "keep it real"; he was able to talk to people like they'd been friends for years. He could relate and did not come across as offensive in his Christian preaching.

Judah told me he had just flown in from his home in Seattle and talked about how he was a die-hard Seahawks fan, joking that since Dallas Cowboys quarterback Tony Romo was also a wedding guest, he would have to forgo his usual ritual and not "pray hard" for him to fail. "I'll get points with God for that, so it's OK," he joked.

When servers began urging guests to make their way to the

assigned tables, Judah patted me between the shoulder blades. "You should come to the Bible study sometime."

"I know," I replied. "Jason's invited me a million times and I plan to." I laughed, adding, "But I guess I'm getting old and lazy."

"Hey, no worries," he said. "We'd love to have ya."

Laziness wasn't the real reason. Instead, I never felt motivated or comfortable with the idea of hanging out in Beverly Hills late on a Wednesday after work to attend a Bible study. I respected those who believed the Bible as a book of divine truth, but I still didn't believe. I had made up my mind some time ago that the Bible was fine to be read, but not to be believed in as divine. So I closed myself off to it. My position seemed perfectly logical, especially as a journalist. I learned from a career of ferreting out reality from rumor how stories could get distorted and even fictionalized as so-called facts were shared from one person to another. I had learned when someone tells me, "I heard Miley Cyrus had sex onstage with a bear," that by the time I get to the real story I will find out Miley only French-kissed a stuffed teddy bear. But more than my suspicions over the Bible's veracity as an accurate historical document, I disagreed with so many things in it—from its anti-gay edicts, to the Armageddon scare tactics in Revelation, to all the crazy talk about foreskins and walking on water and bushes spontaneously combusting. Frankly, I just found the Bible a little too much to be taken seriously as the literal Word of God.

Despite all these prejudices, I had two close members of my family become "born again" and, seemingly, it brought them happiness and comfort. But that history was a very complicated

one that made me feel anything but comfortable going to a
Bible study.

I have four brothers. Three older (the pastor, Kevin; Keith,
a restaurant manager; and Kyle, a marine biologist) and one
younger, Kris, who is a pro-hockey scout). The fact that we
siblings have names starting with a *K* is pretty much the only
thing my family has in common with the Kardashians. We
grew up middle class in a suburb south of Buffalo called Ham-
burg, aka "The Gateway to the South Towns." As kids we
all went to Catholic services, made our First Communion,
with weekly attendance mandated by my mom, who remains
a devout churchgoer today in her seventies. My father, however, never professed to be religious. Sure, he would go to
church with our family, attend the baptisms, and during sermons he would sit quietly in the pew fidgeting while thinking
about how badly he wanted to go outside and have a cigarette.
Though he usually attended, Dad often would spend the car
ride home afterward talking about how most of the parishioners were "hypocrites" who thought they were better than
everyone else when, in fact, they were just as messed up as
anyone else. Churchgoing clearly was something he did out of
duty to please my mother and to give his five kids a foundation
in some sort of faith, even if he didn't believe a lick of it.

After my parents divorced when I was eleven, my father
defiantly proclaimed he would "never step foot inside a church
again." From his pulpit (usually the couch or the driver's seat
of his car), Dad said "Bible thumpers" who believed in Jesus
were the equivalent of adults who believed in Santa Claus.

Not seeing any verifiable proof of a God, or of Jesus, Dad rejected Christianity on the basis that it insulted his intelligence.

So when my oldest brother, Kevin, went from battling drug abuse in his teens to becoming a born-again Christian at age twenty, and followed that up by announcing he was moving to Missouri to attend a Bible college, my father viewed Kevin's dramatic conversion basically as a cautionary tale about "the stupid things people do when drugs fry their brain." Dad didn't proclaim himself an atheist, but he certainly was defiantly agnostic.

Kevin, however, didn't let his lack of paternal spiritual support stop him from founding a fundamentalist Christian church back in Buffalo and home-schooling his four kids partly because he didn't want them too exposed to secular culture. Dad thought my brother ran his family like a cult. Whenever Kevin and his family pulled into his driveway packed into their beat-up Ford sedan, Dad, always an armchair comedian, would quip, "Here come the Ford Lords."

Even so, Kevin frequently invited me, my father, and my brothers, to come to one of his Sunday services. My family never went. Despite becoming "born again," the rest of my family still saw Kevin as the drug-taking, violence-prone bully he was prior and found his makeover unconvincing, even inauthentic. Dad even once put a fist up to Kevin's face and threatened to punch him if he didn't stop trying to recruit him to his church (Kevin could be overbearing to the point of obnoxious). But I had a more nuanced take. A part of me felt bad for Kevin. Here he was, trying to turn his life around, and he found a set of beliefs that gave him the strength to do that. I didn't agree with his literal interpretation of scripture, but at least he no longer dealt drugs out of his apartment.

I was in high school and had stopped going to church on any regular basis a few years earlier when my mother, with whom I was primarily living, let me decide whether playing my hockey games or going to church was more important (hockey won). But when I was sixteen, I accepted Kevin's invitation and went to one of his Sunday-morning services. It was the first time I had ever attended a non-Catholic church and Kevin's was a branch of the Vineyard Christian Fellowship, hard-core in its adherence to the Bible. Kevin preached his sermon to the few dozen church members packed into a hotel ballroom. When Kevin led the group in a song, several members raised their hands to the ceiling and gyrated—and a couple even spoke in tongues (gibberish basically, from what I could tell, that I had only seen on those crazy-seeming Pentecostal services on television). Thank God, no one handled snakes. But it was the kind of raucous religious atmosphere where you'd expect that to happen.

Near the end of the service, Kevin asked the congregation to bow their heads and pray.

"If anyone feels the Holy Spirit within them and wants to commit himself to Jesus today, please step forward and pray with me," Kevin said earnestly, with a vaguely Southern accent, even though this was upstate New York. After pausing, he added, "Right here. Today! Now! You can accept Jesus Christ as your Lord and savior. All your sins will be forgiven."

I cracked open my eyes to see a teenage girl shuffling to the front and kneeling. Kevin put his hands on her head and prayed over her. "Anyone else who wants to accept Jesus, feel free to join us," Kevin then said softly into the microphone.

Being what appeared to be the only other first-timer in my brother's church, I took that as an indirect message to me. But

I didn't step forward. Instead, I just pinched shut my eyes and pretended to pray, though I was more just hoping he would get to the part where they passed around a donation basket so I could soon go home.

I believed in God, always did. But did I believe in a Christian God? The theatrics of the service turned me off. I felt like I was already "born" once and didn't need to do it again. I had been baptized and made my First Communion at St. Bernadette's Church, which, according to Catholic doctrine, was foundational enough.

The next day in my dad's kitchen, he laughed as I retold my experience, especially the part about the spastic movements of the members, the gyrating, and so on.

"Did he walk on water too?" he cracked.

"No, but, seriously, you should go sometime," I told him. "You know, just support him and stuff. It was interesting."

Dad shrugged. "Yeah, well, so is *Seinfeld*. I'll just let him do his thing. I don't want to be a hypocrite. It's all fairy tale."

That was the summer of 1985. But by December of 1994, Larry Baker found himself in a vastly different place spiritually—and physically. Ten months earlier, while I was in grad school at Columbia, Dad had been diagnosed with terminal lung cancer and in a matter of a few months the disease had spread to virtually every bone in his withering body. His heart was failing and his lungs filling with fluid. He wore an oxygen mask virtually 24/7. Tumors had spread throughout his entire body and he spent the majority of the day zonked out on painkillers. Dad refused to do another round of chemo and insisted he would never die in a hospital and would stay home until the end. His doctors told my brothers they were shocked he was still alive.

I was living an eight-hour drive south of Buffalo working as a reporter for a newspaper in southern Virginia, but I would get updates on his condition from my brothers and, whenever my father was coherent, I would talk to him. He didn't have much to say, so I would tell him about what stories I was working on at the newspaper and my attempts at having fun fishing, boating, and exploring the Chesapeake Bay. By all accounts, the end was near, and Dad knew it.

By this time, Pastor Kevin had built up his church to several hundred members and was enjoying a successful career as a preacher. But Kevin had long ago learned not to bring up God or Jesus or any religious "Santa Claus" crap around my dad. So Kevin, rather craftily, sent over the Rev. Tim Black, a friend of his from Big Tree Wesleyan Church, which was located just down the street from my father's duplex.

After meeting with my father, Pastor Black called Kevin. "Your dad is very open spiritually," he said. "You should come pray with him."

Considering past attempts to minister to my father, Kevin had reservations, but as a pastor and son he felt compelled. He found hope in Pastor Black's report, figuring that maybe he could save his father's soul on his deathbed.

On the last Saturday before Christmas, Kevin stopped by my father's place. When he walked into the living room, he saw Dad lying on his side on the couch alone watching TV. His skin looked ashen and his eyes yellow. His breathing was heavy and labored. Dad struggled to sit up when Kevin came in. Tragically, he took off his oxygen mask so that he could light up a cigarette, the very instrument of his demise. Kevin didn't judge him. He was there to love him.

My brother sat in the easy chair beside Dad and chatted with him for a few minutes, just "shooting the bull," as Kevin remembers that visit. Before he left, Kevin asked Dad if he needed anything. "I'm OK," Dad replied, his voice high pitched from his emphysema.

"Dad, you sure you don't want me to pray with you?" Kevin followed. "Just a quick prayer?"

"Yes," he replied with a cough. "That might be good."

Kevin locked his fingers in prayer and asked God if he could provide comfort for my father. He added, "And if it is your will, please heal my father."

To my brother's astonishment and great pleasure, he looked over and saw my fifty-one-year-old father with his eyes closed in prayer. The first time Kevin had ever seen him do so since we were little kids back in church.

Years later, I asked Kevin to tell me more details of this moment with Dad.

"I asked if he wanted to make sure that if his sickness progressed that he was ready to go to God. He said he very much would like to be prepared. So I explained, as any pastor would, that leaving this life is like taking a flight from an airport. We need to be ticketed, then we leave our loved ones at the gate and our flight departs. At our destination there will be loved ones or friends waiting for us to arrive in heaven. Our ticket is praying a simple prayer asking Jesus to forgive us for living a selfish life and asking for a new beginning learning how to live as God intended. I asked if he wanted to tell God something like that in his own words. He said he did. He asked God to forgive him for all the things he did in his life that were not good. He asked for a new beginning, saying, 'I did some pretty shitty things in my life, but I also tried to do good things too.' I told him that just makes him human and assured him that God had heard and that he forgives him. That is the power of Jesus."

When I reach the glass doors to the Four Seasons hotel, where the weekly service is held inside a ballroom, I stop to check my phone, scanning work emails about various celeb dramas I've been covering today. Caitlyn Jenner is feuding with the Kardashians, Matt Damon ticked off the LGBT community with insensitive comments, Donald Trump is mad at *Fox News*—again. I remain eye-buried in my phone, not entirely out of keen interest but also in an effort to distract myself from the anxiety-inducing act I am about to commit. For the first time since my visit to my brother Kevin's church, I am going to an evangelical service. But not just any service. It's the Bible study hosted by Judah Smith.

"Is there a Bible study this week?" I had asked Jason in the newsroom earlier in the week.

Jason's eyes brightened. "Yes!" he said excitedly. "You want to come?"

"Actually, yeah," I said. "I do."

"Cool," Jason said. "I'll save you a seat, buddy."

Jason possesses a goofy, cornball quality that, along with a love of makeup and hair products, makes him come across like a born-again Ron Burgundy. But Jason also is one of the most earnest, honest, and caring male news hosts I've ever worked with. No offense to Ryan Seacrest, but Jason is just a very genuine, sweet guy you can't help but like. And he's also the de facto don of young Hollywood's Christian mafia.

The interesting thing about Jason is that he never pushes

his faith on me and I never really bring up the subject of my beliefs—until now.

My best explanation for why, after being so anti-Bible (not to mention anti–Bible *study* for so long), I suddenly want to attend, is that while I have been lost in my search for God, I see how much strength Jason finds in his faith. I am not necessarily seeking Jesus, but I want to challenge my long-held assumption that the Bible deserves as much respect as a Doritos label. I am curious about whether going in with an open mind will allow me to have a more positive, enriching, and maybe even uplifting experience. In fact, I envy Jason. He reads the Bible every day, once told me he prays hundreds of times a day, and Jesus is his life "copilot." I wouldn't mind feeling the kind of spiritual peace Jason feels, and, with all due respect to my father, I don't want to wait until I am weeks from certain death before having an open mind to it.

But as I step through the hotel doors my stomach is tied into a knot of nerves. What if everyone is a total Jesus freak? What if they ask me to read a passage? What if Judah starts to pray the devil out of me and pressures me to accept Jesus as my Lord and savior? I am plagued with what-if anxiety for good reason: This is more or less exactly what had happened to me as a teenager at my brother Kevin's church.

Directly behind the main hotel tower of the Four Seasons sits a stately brick building housing the hotel's spacious ballrooms, flanked by a convoy of Range Rovers, BMWs, and one Ferrari that line the driveway separating the two structures.

"City Church," Judah's Seattle-based church from which he flies down every Wednesday to minister to the Hollywood set, is printed on placards in front of the building's entrance with an arrow pointing to the left. I follow a group of Bible studiers

down the hall, noting that every one of them appears to be
in their twenties, maybe early thirties at most. One attractive brunette even looks like the naked woman from Robin
Thicke's "Blurred Lines" video. More than a few women
hanging out in the lobby are in tight skirts halfway up their
thighs and most of the dudes are in jeans and T-shirts, making me, in my button-down shirt, instantly one of the most
formally dressed arriving. This is far from the dress code the
last time I went to a born-again church service. Then again,
that was the 1980s. . . .

As I walk into the ballroom, bass-heavy EDM music blasts
from speakers and the room is set with chairs some twenty
rows deep. I find one near the back on the left aisle and watch
workers tinkering on the lighted stage platform that's filled
with drums, amplifiers, microphones, and guitars perched on
stands like it's a rock concert.

A few minutes later, by eight o'clock, the room is packed
with worshipers, most of whom are engaged in friendly conversation and hugging and carrying on in a way that belies
the usual standoffish demeanor you find around town. It was
like being at a young Hollywood cocktail party—but without
the booze and beautiful people acting lame and aloof. These
church people genuinely look happy, including Jason and Lauren, who I see from my hideout sitting front and center by the
stage.

Out of habit after twenty years of celebrity reporting, I scan
the crowd for famous people. I already know Justin Bieber
won't be here, as I just saw paparazzi photos of him in Asia
earlier today. But several attendees are too familiar-looking
not to be famous—or at least *almost* famous. Then, as I am
trying to figure out if the petite blonde is Brittany Snow from

the *Pitch Perfect* movies, I see a skinny blond woman with very long legs in tight blue jeans walking down my aisle, her hair cutely tied up in a topknot: Gwen Stefani. I have interviewed Gwen before and have seen her live in concert with her band, No Doubt, several times. Confession: I am a fan. OK, fine, in full disclosure: Gwen used to be my celebrity crush—before I became so turned off by narcissistic celebrities I stopped having any. Yet admittedly, seeing Gwen take a seat a few rows in front of me, choosing to be at the same service, makes my attendance feel more, I don't know, justified or something. I'm not proud of this sensation I am having. I am a living, breathing, fanboy-ing personification of why celebrities can be so influential on others. I am thinking, If Gwen Stefani thinks this Bible study is cool then, hey . . . I wish I could say I don't feel validated by her, but—lame alert!—I really do feel validated. I am a sucker just like the rest of celebrity-obsessed Americans.

As I drink in Gwen's arrival, a burly young guy in a polo shirt comes up to me.

"I'm Greg," he says, shaking my hand with a jerk up and down. "You've been here before?"

"No, it's my first time," I reply. "You?"

"I've been coming for a few months—you're gonna love it, man. I hope Judah shows. He's such a genuine guy."

"Judah might not be here?" I ask with concern. After all, I didn't come here to see some random preacher. "I thought he led this service every Wednesday."

"Well, sometimes he can't make it," Greg explains. "But I think he'll be here tonight."

Greg tells me he's from Virginia, an actor, and that he moved to L.A. a year ago to follow his Hollywood acting dreams.

I ask him how that's working out for him. "Oh, there are

a lot of highs and lows," he says with a shrug. "But it's all a blessing."

I encourage Greg to stick with it and give him a friendly pat on the shoulder. As Greg takes a seat in front of me, my phone blings alive with a text alert.

you here? We saved you a seat.

It's Jason. The polite thing to do is to reply. But I am afraid he will invite me up front. I want to stay near the back and take it all in on my own, away from Judah's and Jason's gazes. You know, just in case things turn too Bible-y and whatnot.

Thankfully, the band starts playing an uplifting song, everyone takes to their feet, and minutes later, Judah bounds onto the stage in a pair of black skinny jeans, a light-gray T-shirt, and a stylish dark sport coat and he's clutching a black Bible. He looks like the host of an MTV game show.

"For those of you who've been here, welcome back," Judah shouts out. "For those of you here for the first time, you're probably thinking, This looks less like a Bible study and more like a full-blown church experience. But rest easy, be at ease. We won't be sacrificing any animals tonight."

The crowd laughs. And I feel at ease. This guy is good at what he does. He really knows how to read a room.

"I am a Jesus guy," he continues. "But this is a zero-pressure zone."

Hallelujah!

After he thanks "my good friend Jason" for starting the Bible study group a few years ago inside a house in the Hollywood

Hills, and then cracks a few jokes (including how he liked to get his real news from *E! News*, saying, "I like to watch Kardashians reruns and veg out"), Judah, the pop-culture preacher, launches into his sermon. "I want to talk about that question that plagues all of us: 'What's really going on?' You watch the news. You see all the wars, the missiles, the pestilence, the political races. But I want to talk about what's really happening on the Earth."

He opens his Bible. Then, he stops abruptly and stares at the crowd through his thick lenses. "No worries if you don't have a Bible. I brought one for you. It's all good."

Chuckling along with the crowd, the natural showman begins reading from Psalm 24, which was written, he explains, by David, whom he calls "an average but extraordinary dude" who helped write the Bible, or what Judah describes as "an inspired guide to human existence."

Judah reads the first line of the Psalm: "The Earth is the Lord's and the fullness thereof, the world and those who dwell therein." He puts the Bible down and gushes, "Well, that's a pretty radical start to a Psalm! David says all the Earth belongs to God. He breathed it into existence and hand made it *all by himself*! All the animals, all the humans are his design. Everything!" Judah shakes his head. "So that pretty much is letting us know who's the boss."

All those hours of my childhood spent listening to my Catholic priest drone on and on like the teacher in *Ferris Bueller's Day Off* never engaged me even close to the level of this gifted thirtysomething storyteller.

"God cares about you," Judah goes on. "He cares about what you do. So whatever you do, we must do it for the glory of God. You can take your acting career, your good looks, your personality, your fashion skills, you can do it for His glory. Do it for the Big Picture. If you're a barista at Starbucks, do it for God. It doesn't matter what you do. He cares about everything you do."

Judah is obviously playing to his audience of performers and personalities (including me), and his message speaks to something not so ineffable in me. Lately, I have begun suffering from a crisis of sorts, questioning what deeper purpose or meaning I find in my work. I get paid to go on TV and talk about famous people. What's the point in that? Isn't it all just so meaningless and superficial? Shouldn't I be doing something more important with my life? Not necessarily, according to Judah, who suggests God even cares about *E! News*. After all, God, Judah would say, "breathed" my career into existence, because I am His "son" and He is my "father." That's partly what I have been seeking: How to find meaning in everyday modern life.

Even though it is a message being tailored to Hollywood types like me, what with our tendency to [breaking news alert!] score higher than average on the narcissism scale, it makes sense and, well, makes me feel better about myself.

Twenty minutes into his sermon, Judah has the crowd entirely rapt. "Look, folks. Whatever you do, do it with a sense of conviction and confidence that God has your back. Do it with consideration of others before yourself, with an attitude of a servant. And do it with thankfulness and gratitude. What you do matters to God."

Now sweating from all his stomping across the stage, Judah repeats that this is a "zero-pressure zone," but he says anyone who wishes to accept Jesus tonight can do so right now and pray.

Just as it was some thirty years before, I don't join in the silent prayer to accept Jesus. But unlike that previous experience at my brother's church, I do feel better, more grounded, more relaxed, and more purposeful than when I walked in. In a sense, I feel a bit healed. It's as if I feel less alone, more significant, and more . . . loved.

Near the end of the hour-long service, when the band starts playing a celebratory song with a rock beat, I open my eyes and see Gwen Stefani walking hurriedly up the aisle toward the exit. She has tears in her eyes and wipes them as she looks down at the floor. I try not to get busted, but celebrities in the wild are a lot like car wrecks on the freeway: You can't help but stare. Suddenly, as she is just a few feet from me in the aisle, Gwen looks up. My brown eyes lock with her blues. But this moment won't be a soul connection. Instead, Gwen self-consciously darts her eyes forward, and I do the same, seeing her pass by in my periphery as the rest of the congregation dutifully has their eyes shut as instructed. I am such an idiot.

After the band stops and Judah ends the service with "God bless you all!" I step through the mingling crowd to the front to give Jason and Lauren a hug, thanking them for inviting me and explaining that I had found a seat already when they texted. "No problem, buddy," Jason says, guiding me over to Judah, whose forehead is still glistening from his preacher's workout. I can't say that Judah converted me into being a born-again Christian, or that he has made me believe the Bible is truly in fact the word of the One True God, but I do feel as if . . . well, something spiritual has just happened.

"How'd you like it?" Judah asks me.

"Honestly, I loved it. I feel more . . ." I fear I will offend him if I say the wrong thing. "I feel more connected to God."

Judah wraps me in a one-armed bro hug. "Great to hear, my man! That's what it's all about. Making that connection stronger."

"Seriously, thank you," I add. "You've got a gift. I enjoyed it."

"That means a lot," Judah says. "You're welcome to come back anytime."

I don't feel reborn. I didn't just accept Jesus into my heart in this swanky hotel ballroom with a cast of cool-kid Christians. But the experience was enlightening, informative, uplifting, and soul-nourishing enough for me to look Judah in the eyes, shake his hand, and promise, "I definitely will be back."

At the time, I had no way of knowing just how unusual my road back to Judah's Bible study would be.

V

CELEBRATE JESUS—HE'S JUST LIKE US!

I appear on *E! News* and *E! Online* five days a week as a professional extrovert—where I analyze, report on, and critique the personal and professional lives of famous people, performing my public service in stylish clothes and perfectly coiffed hair. It's all a carefully crafted production that celebrates the good, the bad, and the ugly of Hollywood life.

Yet when I leave the E! studios and drive the hour (or more) on the freeway back home to Hermosa Beach, I retreat into my sweatpants and a T-shirt and I like to read, write, relax, ride my bike by the beach, and generally stay out of other people's business. Or, when in hockey-dad mode, you'll find me at an ice rink watching my kids with a hoodie pulled over my head, white earbud wires dangling beside my cheeks, the portrait of an antisocial personality.

I'm what you'd call dichotomous. And it's a balance I mostly like about myself. It's also a big reason why I have always gotten along so well with another Hollywood personality—the matriarch of the Kardashian-Jenner empire, Kris Jenner.

Kris flaunts her materialistic celebrity lifestyle, residing in a mansion in the ritzy gated community of Hidden Hills, flying around the world in private jets, driving her Rolls-Royce in her designer shades, and carrying handbags worth more money than some Americans make in a year. Yet as I have gotten to know Kris better over the last ten years, I've learned that she also is a deeply spiritual mother, loving grandmother, and a badass businesswoman who gains her strength from a dedicated, genuine relationship with God that includes weekly church attendance.

Kris and I met in early 2006, some two years before the Kardashians would become America's First (reality-TV) Family upon the launch of E!'s *Keeping Up with the Kardashians*. Back then, I was an editor for *Us Weekly* and had driven up to Calabasas to interview her daughter Kim, who had just gained attention for having a brief fling with Jessica Simpson's ex-husband, Nick Lachey. Kris and I instantly hit it off. We gossiped about various celebrities, and I served as a sounding board for different ideas she had to boost her husband Bruce Jenner's career. At that first meeting, Kris even tried to set me up with her oldest daughter, Kourtney . . . until she found out I was recently married.

Soon, I had a front-row seat to the family's subsequent rise to the top of the famousphere, regularly interviewing family members and breaking exclusive news about their various adventures. In 2008, I joined E! full-time and my relationship to the family grew even closer and more personal. I attended their birthday parties, housewarming parties, weddings, dinner parties at the family home (yes, they love to throw parties); flew to Las Vegas to party with them; even brought my family to Kris's annual Christmas Eve party, a soiree featuring elves serving Willy Wonka–like candies in a huge tent decorated like a winter wonderland. The night ended with a visit from the "real Santa Claus," who placed kids on his lap and handed personal gifts to every child. One year, I got to see Kim and Kanye West proudly snap photos of their infant daughter North's first sitting upon Santa's knee (yes, she cried).

Through it all, Kris, who is fifteen years older than me, has become a friend, confidante, and mentor. I will often seek her advice on various issues. Through the paparazzi and reality-TV lenses, Kris may appear to be a self-absorbed pagan, but in real life she is anything but that. Like a lot of things in Hollywood, appearances are deceiving when it comes to Kris Jenner.

Yet despite my coziness with the Kards, as some fans affectionately call them, I have never gone to church with them, though they regularly attend Christian services near their home at a small, nondenominational church (to which Kris donates 10 percent of her annual income, a tithe) founded by a charismatic pastor who has appeared on their reality show many times, the Rev. Brad Johnson.

My first Wednesday-night Bible study with Judah went surprisingly well, breaking down at least a few bricks in the wall that has separated me from the Bible. But I feel like I need to find a pastor with whom I can develop a relationship, in a church I can go to on Sundays and figure out if churchgoing will lead me down a path to finding God.

A week after attending Judah's Bible study, I see on the in-house shooting schedule for the E! studios that Kris has a promotional shoot in our building. As soon as I get to work, I walk down to the makeup room on the first floor to say hello.

"Hey, Ken!" Kris says from her chair as I part her entourage.

She leans in for a hug and kisses me on the cheek. "We haven't talked in a while," she says with a smile.

"Yeah, it's been about two days," I reply.

"Well." Kris laughs. "That's a long time for us!"

I stand next to Kris and we look at each other in the mirror as her makeup artist, Joyce, finishes up her glam touch-ups. After some chitchat about how fast her teenage daughters, Kendall and Kylie, are growing up; about how much better Lamar is doing now that he survived his overdose several months back (I haven't yet told her how much his health crisis helped spark my spiritual journey); I ask her how often she goes to Pastor Brad's church.

"Every Sunday," she says. "As long as I'm in town—or not working."

"Can I come with you sometime?" I ask.

"Of course, Ken! You can come anytime."

"How about this Sunday?" I ask. "Will you be there?"

I would feel awkward going alone.

"I'll check my schedule," Kris says. "But that should work. You will love it. Brad is the man!"

I have never met Pastor Brad, but I am familiar with his story. Turns out that before Brad Johnson became "the man," the charismatic preacher had to undergo a personal resurrection as dramatic as any Hollywood comeback I've ever seen.

Around the time I met the Kardashian family in the late 2000s, Brad led the 4,000-member congregation at Calvary Community Church in the upscale L.A. suburb of Westlake Village. The Kards were among the megachurch's many famous members.

Then, in 2007, a tabloid-ready scandal struck the church. But this one had nothing to do with its most scandalous family. Rather, this tale starred its ever-smiling and charming leader with a thick head of golden-brown hair, who shocked the congregation by confessing publicly that he had been cheating on his wife with another woman. He later wrote in a blog post: "I am sorry for the pain and emotional upheaval my actions have caused you and the precious bride of Christ. I'm sorry for the deceptions, the irresponsibility, and the sin of adultery that came from my life and infected others. I assume full responsibility for my actions with no excuses and no rationalizations."

Brad's indiscretion resulted in the end of his twenty-seven-year marriage, and seemingly his pastoral career. He fell into a spiral hauntingly similar to that of Lamar Odom, whose wedding to Khloe Kardashian Brad officiated (in front of E! reality cameras). Brad fell into clinical depression and, sadly, even attempted to kill himself three times. One time, paramedics rushed to his home after it was reported that he had overdosed. He survived—but barely.

Brad focused on his faith in Christ and prayed daily for forgiveness. He also went on antidepressants to help pull him from his psychological abyss.

Then he got a new job, as a barista at Starbucks.

While working for minimum wage pouring coffee, Brad was almost quite literally stalked by Kris and Bruce Jenner, who had been looking for him for several months. The couple had since left Calvary and, along with other like-minded former members, wanted to start a new church. Their choice for pastor: Brad Johnson.

"When I found out he was working at Starbucks I couldn't believe it," Kris told me. "Not that there is necessarily any shame in working at Starbucks, but I was like, Brad needs to be leading a church. I felt that his mistakes, and his persecution by the old church, would make him a better pastor. It was his shot at redemption. I couldn't think of a better person to lead the church. Nobody is perfect."

⚓

Days later, as I head to the front door to leave for Kris Jenner's church, my wife, Brooke, is standing in the kitchen and jokes, "Say hi to Jesus if you see him."

Even if she did not think the idea of finding divine inspiration at a church founded by a reality-TV star was a potentially silly one, I certainly wouldn't want her, and not the kids either to come with me on this church visit. After all, the experience could be a bad one and could turn them off. So I go alone.

I pull in right before the ten a.m. service is set to start. When I walk through the glass doors of Pastor Brad's church, the first thing I notice is a box of black-and-white rubber bracelets on which is printed, NO PERFECT PEOPLE ALLOWED. I'm early, so the sparse sanctuary, which sits in a strip mall near the 101 Freeway, is still half empty as I enter and an usher hands one to me. As I am sliding the bracelet onto my wrist, a thin blond woman comes up to me.

"Kris told me to look out for you!" she says, shaking my hand and flashing a big smile. "I'm Karen, Brad's wife."

"Nice to meet you," I say.

"Come back here and meet Brad."

Karen guides me to the rear of the space and pushes open a door to a meeting room, where Brad is sitting at a conference table going over his sermon notes.

Upon seeing me, Brad bounds to his feet. "Hey, Ken! I heard you might be coming."

"I'm here," I reply. "Where's Kris?"

"Oh, I guess she had a shoot today for the Oscars," Karen explains.

Actually, I knew this. But I forgot. She had to appear on the E! pre-show, but lately my mind hadn't been doing a great job of keeping track of much of anything, especially other people's schedules, not to mention I'd just had to beg a publisher to give me another year on a book deadline because . . . why? Because by the time the weekend (when I typically do most of my writing) comes, my brain is so scrambled from managing the stress of my job, my commute, my anxiety, my general state of feeling adrift. In short, I have been overwhelmed. I am here because I desperately need to still my mind, find peace, and have a life grounded in spirituality. Going to church helps a lot of people, including my friend Kris, and Judah's Bible study opened me back up to the Christian message; why not try going to church for real?

"Well, I get you all to myself," I joke to Brad.

"Along with a hundred or so others." He laughs.

Brad has the sleeves of his paisley-print button-down shirt rolled up to his mid-forearm and wears a black NO PERFECT PEOPLE ALLOWED rubber bracelet on his right wrist. He looks like he's a dad dressed "cool" for a Super Bowl party. And Brad is smiling like it's a party.

"Welcome to our humble sanctuary," he says of the former retail space that sits in a strip mall flush against the 101 Freeway, beside a shoe store and a swimming school for kids called Water Wings. And here I sit, front and center, hoping Pastor

Brad can help me swim closer to God—or at least keep me from drowning.

Brad has a round face and teeth that seem wider and whiter than most, which makes him all the more inviting. At Starbucks, Brad must have been the happiest, most blessed barista ever.

"I have been hearing about you for a long time," I tell Brad. "I can't believe we've never met."

"But I feel like we have."

"Yeah, like maybe I saw you at one of Kris's parties."

"Something like that, I am sure of it."

"Let me ask God." I fold my hands in front of my chest in mock prayer (I act goofy when I'm nervous). "Maybe He remembers."

"Good one!" Brad says with a grin. "I'm gonna have to use that one."

Brad is easy to talk to, which seems to be a job prerequisite for preachers these days. They need to be accessible, real people. Brad emanates realness. I can see how Kris Jenner and the family feel comfortable here with Brad. Plus, he's entertaining, earnest, and with the small sanctuary of some 150 seats he provides a sense of privacy every Sunday to otherwise wildly public people. Then, when you factor in that the church's motto is "No Perfect People Allowed," it's clear that a group of people who are criticized daily by online haters and bullies would find this humble little suburban church a welcoming spiritual retreat.

"Well, we hope you enjoy the message today," Brad says, glancing at his notes.

"I'll let you get back to your sermon," I say. "Thanks again for having me."

Brad's wife walks me to the front row, and we sit side by side. "Kris always sits right here," she whispers.

"Is this the VIP section?"

Karen nods and smiles.

Stop being silly, I tell myself.

A four-man soft-rock band warms up the mostly full room, which is neither the grand opulence of Judah's Beverly Hills hotel ballroom or the echo-filled chambers of my Catholic youth. Given that Kris and company are away, there are also no celebrities, no Hollywood insiders, thus I feel like I can just sit and listen and learn and pray. And I like having this space.

When Brad steps behind the lectern, it's just him, his Bible, and a microphone. All the other trappings of some churchgoing experiences—candles, stained-glass windows, marble altars, dramatic lighting—are missing. The sparseness evokes a natural, genuine, welcoming atmosphere. With its low ceiling and carpeted floor, an airy cathedral it is not.

Brad starts off by announcing that for the next four Sundays he will be preaching a series of sermons titled, "Jesus in His Own Words," explaining, "Jesus gave us 'I am' statements. He had seven different descriptions. We are taking on four of them for a month."

Today's sermon, he says gleefully, comes from John 10:11, which reads, "I am the good shepherd. The good shepherd lays down his life for the sheep."

Brad goes on to describe how Jesus often used the metaphor of God as our keeper and caregiver as a shepherd is to his flock. "Sheep are mentioned two hundred times in the Bible," Brad says. "They're the most frequently mentioned animal in the Bible." By comparison, Brad notes, dogs are mentioned forty-four times and cats . . . well, zero times. Being a dog person, and highly allergic to most cats, with this knowledge I am already feeling closer to Jesus.

I glance inside the program that was handed to me on the way in and find that an outline of Brad's sermon is printed on the inside, sort of a Cliff's Notes of his preaching. Wow, if my priests back in Buffalo growing up gave me a read-along guide like this I would have gotten a lot more out of their homilies!

"The Bible says we are sheep," Brad continues. "And sheep aren't necessarily the sharpest knives in the drawer. They are the original possessors of ADD." Brad mimics a wandering sheep bouncing from spot to spot on the stage. "There's some grass, there's some grass." The congregation laughs along with him. "They can't recognize danger ahead of time. They are very hard to lead."

I get what he's saying. Part of the reason I soon will be pushing fifty years old and still don't have a well-defined spiritual belief system is that I get distracted moment by moment by the external ephemera of life (phones, friends, work, sports) rather than stopping, at least for a little bit each day, to seek out God. Sure, modern life makes it a lot harder than it was two thousand years ago, but we are also a hell of a lot more comfortable than they were back then, thus we should have more time and energy to devote to spiritual matters. But most of us don't. I know I don't. I am a sheep.

Brad goes on with the humans-as-sheep metaphor, and he encourages us to glance at today's program where he has printed a summary of his points:

SHEEP GET LOST EASILY.

Pastor Brad stands at the lectern and reads from Isaiah 53, saying, "We like sheep have gone astray." He looks out at the congregation. "We are prone to wander. Our tendency is to get lost. We, like sheep, easily go astray. That's why we need a shepherd."

SHEEP ARE DEFENSELESS.

Smiling, Brad adds, "The best they can do is say baaaack off." Everyone laughs, including Brad.

SHEEP ARE STUBBORN.

"Now everyone is looking at the person next to them and saying, 'He must be talking about you.'" After a quick chuckle, Brad turns serious. "The Bible says that the sheep who go astray, their desire is to do what *they* want rather than what the *shepherd* wants." Brad steps away from the podium and wipes his forehead with his forearm as he relays that sheep are well known to go off on their own and get stuck between rocks, determined to squeeze through without their shepherd, only to die trying to go it alone. "How many of you are determined to work your own way out of it?"

Brad has silenced the congregants, including me, to whom he seems to be directly speaking. He's spot-on that I am Lone Wolf Guy, always insisting I figure things out on my own. Yet this has only left me feeling stuck.

Brad, a man who once was disgraced following a church sex scandal, lets out a sigh.

"Look, my life was a wreck. My life was a mess. A lot of

people confronted me, but I was like Baskin Robbins: Take a number, dude. But then at night I couldn't sleep because what they said went right to my heart. I hadn't turned to the Lord yet. A friend said to me, 'Brad, if it was your best thinking that got you here, what makes you believe that it is your best thinking that can get you out?' That went right to my heart. I decided that I needed a shepherd. I was being very stubborn."

SHEEP ARE DIRTY.

"They are nasty," he says. "They stink, there are flies. They have no ability to wash themselves. And that is the way we are in the mind of God. Without Jesus, without our sins forgiven, the best you can do in the eyes of God is to be nasty. Here is the point: We need a savior like sheep need a shepherd. The Good Shepherd laid down his life for his sheep."

I'm not feeling very warm and fuzzy about the message that I am interpreting, in part, as this: I'm dirty unless God washes me of my sinful ways. That seems a bit harsh to me, a little too 30 AD to my twenty-first-century thinking. I would prefer a more positive message, perhaps like, "We are all clean, but God wipes away the grime when we get dirty." This Almighty God—I imagine: gray-bearded old man standing at heaven's gate with a report card of your sins—is the one I have always resisted and came to resent. But like Brad points out, maybe I am being stubborn. There is some logic to the argument. I mean, where has this God-resistant way of thinking got me? The answer seems to be it got me here to Kris Jenner's church, hanging on every word, hoping to find God amid the noise that is my life.

Brad asks everyone to open to John 10:3–4, and he reads, "The gatekeeper opens the gate for the shepherd and the sheep recognize his voice and come to him. He calls his own by name and leads them out. When he has brought out all his own, he goes on ahead of them, and his sheep follow him because they know his voice."

Brad further explains, "The Bible says we can learn to recognize the voice of God. It doesn't have to be the literal voice, but he speaks through scriptures. The Bible is God's love letter to you. 'This is my direction to you, this is my way, this is the path to follow . . .' If you are not reading the scriptures, you are missing a lot of what God could say to you every single day.

"The pressure is off you. Psalm 23 says, 'Jesus, you guide me and I will follow' . . . He provides for our souls. Some of you right now, it seems like life is going your way, but inside you have an unsettled soul. You have an un-refreshed soul. You don't have peace in your life; you're not sleeping well at night. You're burdened every day. On the outside you've got your smile on, and when you walked in here people smiled at you and said, "Man, you've got a good life." But you know something is wrong inside. You need your soul refreshed."

And in a thirty-second clip of his sermon Brad has summed up my wayward spiritual state of being. I've been taking the sedative Trazodone to sleep at night, I entertain and inform and smile my way through work every day. I know that the real me is a scared little boy who just wants to find equanimity, peace . . . God.

Brad pauses, seemingly sensing his relatable sermon has connected with his flock. He glances down at me and cracks a soft smile before looking up at the congregation. "Some of you right now are facing the consequences of bad decisions you've made. Like, the pain is horrible. It's like somebody took a stick and had at it with you. You feel the pain of your life. Listen, not all pain is a result of sin. But sometimes we've got to ask, *God have you let this pain into my life to correct me? Have you allowed this pain into my life so that I will come closer to you?* When are you more apt to turn to God? When you are hurting or when life is good?"

That last question elicits a murmur of chuckles.

"If there was ever a time in your life when you were closer to Jesus than you are right now, this is a good time for you to come home," Brad says. "This is a good day for you to come back to the Shepherd. This is a good day to say, Yeah I wandered. And I am going to turn my life back and I'm going to talk closely with the Lord one more time."

The stage lights dim and Brad bows his head.

"Let us pray together," he says gently. I bow my head and close my eyes. I fold my hands in prayer, just like at church in the 1970s, as Brad begins his earnest prayer.

"Father, I ask that your Holy Spirit would begin to speak to us right now and transform people's hearts right now. Who here would say, 'I am a sheep and I need the care of a shepherd'? Who would say that in your heart? Who's here this morning and would say, 'I have decisions to make and I need my shepherd to guide me'? Some of you would say, 'Brad, right now I am empty. I need the shepherd to be my provider— maybe materially, maybe spiritually. You need peace. Who here would say, 'I used to be very close to Christ and I've wandered away like a sheep'? And I wanna come home and I wanna come back to him? You can do that right now. And

I pray that no one leaves today without knowing the Good Shepherd. In Jesus's name, we pray. Can I get an amen?"

"Amen!" I say. And I mean it.

Brad then asks anyone in the church today who is ready to accept Jesus Christ as their Lord and savior to stand up. This call to accept is standard fare in most nondenominational Christian churches, as I learned from my brother Kevin. The act of professing your faith in Jesus as a way to ensure an infinite place in heaven is at the core of Christian faith. As John 3:16 states: "For God so loved the world that he gave his one and only Son, that whoever believes in him shall not perish but have eternal life."

Despite the nurturing thought of not having to sweat the small stuff because I will be happy in heaven if I accept Jesus in my heart, I remain seated. Like at Judah's Bible study, I feel as though the biblical message Brad has shared is relevant, relatable, and is bringing me closer to God—but not so close that I am willing to commit my soul exclusively to Jesus Christ. Could I use a shepherd in my life? Absolutely. Is it going to come only through Christianity? Maybe. But I haven't examined enough to know. Still, so far, I see no reason why Christianity, and its uplifting message of redemption, can't be part of my path to spiritual healing. So I remain on the fence. At this stage, to do anything else would be dishonest. But I am enjoying this celebration, even if I might conclude that Jesus Christ represents nothing more than the notion that we can all be reborn no matter how much we mess things up. There's a well-worn adage that says "Hollywood loves a comeback." But really, when it comes to ourselves, we all do.

Afterward, Brad stands at the exit shaking hands with everyone as they leave to their cars.

"Thanks for coming, Ken!" Brad tells me as I pass by. "Let's chat more about this search of yours sometime. Just give me a call."

I promise him I will and shake his hand. Brad looks into my eyes for an awkwardly long time. He knows I have pain I haven't shared. And so do I. Today is not the day to share it. I am not ready.

Nonetheless, I wave goodbye and leave the church feeling way more at peace and mindful than when I entered. Progress. I decide to give myself homework: Read the entire Book of John, from which Brad was reading today. So I drive through the Santa Monica Mountains to Malibu and sit outside a coffee shop as rich hipsters shuffle in and out in their beach sandals.

John, along with Matthew, Mark, and Luke, is one of the four Gospels of the New Testament. Tradition holds that John, known as the beloved disciple and one of Jesus's original twelve followers, wrote his Gospel in twenty-one action-packed chapters around 90 AD and recalls his firsthand, eyewitness account of Jesus's life. With caffeine buzzing through my system, I rifle through the chapters and verses . . .

> He was in the beginning with God; all things were made through him, and without him was not anything made that was made. In him was life, and the life was the light of men. The light shines in the darkness, and the darkness has not overcome it . . . For God so loved the world that he gave his only Son, that whoever believes in him should not perish but have eternal life. . . . Let him who is without sin among you be the first to throw a stone at her . . . I am the door; if any one enters by me, he will be saved . . . I did not come to judge the world but to

save the world . . . Love one another, even as I have loved you . . .

The Bible isn't just a book, it's sort of a screenplay, chock full of entertaining and informative stories. While as a kid I got the impression that the stories were about these boring old guys from a long, long time ago, I realize that, as Brad preached, the stories are really about us. For me, they're not so much literal as they are allegorical. In this Cecil B. DeMille–like biblical production, we are supposed to see ourselves. I'm reminded of when I was working as an editor at *Us Weekly* back in 2002, and my editor in chief, Bonnie Fuller, asked me what I thought about a new photo section she wanted to start called "Stars—They're Just Like Us!" featuring paparazzi photos showing famous people doing everyday things.

"It's brilliant," I said. "People read our magazine to see themselves." And that's why I am reading the Bible. I want to see myself. And I do. I know that the Bible is the all-time bestselling book, but I bet sales would really skyrocket if it was renamed *Jesus—He's Just Like Us!*

As the caffeine buzz begins to wear off, I check my phone and see a text from Kris Jenner.

how was church w brad?

very good. I like him a lot!

yay!! come next Sunday and ill be there. How r u doing?

honestly, feeling a little lost.

God knows I know what that's like and it's super tough ...
I'm happy brad brings you some comfort and that you can

come to a feeling of peace thru a relationship with him and us and God and prayer … I'm here for you if you ever need me … Just one day at a time … And breathe.…

Breathe.

It was like Kris was with me earlier that morning. I actually could breathe while in church. My chest didn't feel tight. My thoughts weren't racing. I felt calm.

If only life were lived within the four walls of a church, I could feel strong enough to face anything. But real life is far more challenging when you go home and don't have a pastor of positivity wrapping a "Jesus Loves You" blanket around you.

VI

MEDITATE IN MARINA DEL REY

She has blond hair, blue eyes, a tiny nose, high cheekbones, flawless tanned skin, and a slim build with broad shoulders that flare down in a V-shape to her waist, where long legs stretch to the ground. Her physicality isn't what comes to mind when I envision an oracle. But I have come to visit her in the hope that she is one.

So while most people spotting a tank-top-clad Brittany Daniel walking in flip-flops across her condominium courtyard in Marina del Rey might see a genetically blessed actress, I see something less obvious. In Brittany, I see a vision of death—and that's why I have come to see her.

"Hey!" she says, greeting me with a hug, holding on extra long. When she lets go, I hold her by the outside of her arms and scan her.

"You look great!" I say.

"Thank you," Brittany replies, looking shyly down at the ground.

I'm not handing her a hollow Hollywood compliment.

Given what she has endured, the fact that she is alive, let alone looking so tan and healthy, is a miracle.

A former teen star from her days as a cheerleader (with her twin sister) on the mid-1990s TV show *Sweet Valley High*, Brittany had gone on to a successful acting career as an adult, something not very easy to do. I've seen so many young stars struggle to make the transition, but she did. Brittany starred in the show *Dawson's Creek*, famously played David Spade's girlfriend in the two *Joe Dirt* movies, made *Stuff* magazine's list of the "Hottest Women in the World" and hilariously nailed her role with the Wayans brothers in *White Chicks*.

By the time I met her in 2007, Brittany had joined the cast of the popular sitcom *The Game*. A reporter who worked with me at *Us Weekly* had introduced us because Brittany, as much an athlete as an actress, was putting together a team to compete in a celebrity triathlon in Malibu. Brittany invited me to join. At the time, my hockey-injured hip had not yet grown too stiff and I could run four days a week, so I agreed to do the race. We were never super-close friends, but we trained together a few times with the team and got along really well.

Most actors tend to be typecast, a product of casting directors who look at actors sort of like a cup of Starbucks coffee: They want to know exactly what they're gonna taste every time. In Brittany's case, her type had become the sexy, sassy blonde.

But in real life Brittany was thoughtful, introverted, and far from a little sassy pants. She was always interested in my brain tumor, how I overcame it, and expressed a lot of support for me overcoming it and being so open about my experience. She even appeared at some events I held to raise money for a charity I had started for brain-tumor survivors. I went on to work at *E! News* and ran into Brittany a few times at some charity events and parties, where she was always kind and genuine, but otherwise I didn't see her very often. Yet such is the Hollywood lifestyle. I liken it to riding an elevator and at each floor some people get on and off, but you stay on. You might work with someone on a project for a few months and be close friends, but then never see them again after it wraps. The fact that I have had the same daily workplace at E! for almost ten years is quite rare. Most performers and media professionals operate in a series of temporary work situations akin to one-night stands.

In 2011, Brittany got a blood test done hoping to find out why she had constant flu-like symptoms, night sweats, and why her lower back hurt so bad she couldn't sit for any extended period of time without coming to tears in pain. She assumed she had a virus and could get some medicine and move on with it. Instead, the tests came back positive for cancer. Brittany, at age thirty-four, found out she had stage IV non-Hodgkins lymphoma. Malignant tumors filled her abdominal cavity and had already spread throughout her body into her lymph nodes.

When I heard the bad news from our mutual friend, Heather, I called and texted Brittany several times for weeks. She never replied.

"Why won't Brittany return my calls?" I finally asked Heather.

"She's probably just overwhelmed," Heather said. "She just needs time to process everything."

Or maybe, I feared, she was just afraid I would want to report the news, which she had been keeping private. It's a job hazard when you're a journalist in this town, where many times I have thought I was a "friend" of a celebrity only to find out they always saw me more as a reporter.

I kept track of her progress through Heather. *She had surgery last week . . . another round of chemo . . . she's cancer-free.* But Britt and I hadn't talked since her diagnosis. Here was a survivor, someone who had endured a life-threatening illness. In my experience, people who stare death in the face and live to tell about it come back with spiritual insights and perspectives others don't have. They are gifts to the rest of us; they are living resources.

So, nearly five years after her diagnosis, I have reached out to Brittany at a time when I am not letting my fears keep me from reaching out to people.

"Let's walk up to my place," Brittany tells me, closing the courtyard gate. "I ordered some food for us."

I follow her up the stairs to her two-bedroom condo overlooking the marina. It's a sunny spring afternoon and the sea air blows in through the sliding glass windows from her balcony. I settle down on the couch as she makes tea in the kitchen, updating me on how she has been working on a reality-show idea and spending time just chilling with her new boyfriend and is hoping to get engaged. After spending the last few years fighting for her life, now she's able to enjoy it.

"So how've *you* been, Mr. Baker?" she asks.

"Honestly, I've had a lot of anxiety. I mean, a lot. I just feel, like, totally unanchored and stressed."

Britt's forehead furrows with concern. "I'm sorry, Ken. What's stressing you out?"

"Lately? Seems like everything. I worry nonstop. About the kids, about work stuff, about my marriage, about my health."

"Have you seen a doctor?" she asks.

"Yes," I say, uncomfortable that this interview has turned on to me. "Just had a physical and everything checks out fine."

"So it's a mental thing?"

"Sort of, yeah. I guess so." I sigh. "But I think it's deeper than that. I've gone to a therapist and we talk about all sorts of stuff. It helps. But what I've realized is that the source of my problem is much deeper, it's much more on a spiritual level. You know?"

Britt nods supportively. "They say anxiety is an emotion that comes from fear," she says. "So what most scares you?"

I shake my head.

"Why are you shaking your head?" she asks.

"Because I feel so silly talking about being scared to someone who had cancer."

"But facing your fears helps you overcome them," she says. "I was very scared of cancer. But I faced it. Now I am not. So tell me, Ken, what scares you the most?"

"I'm scared of dying, being alone, getting sick." I look up at heaven and nothing at the same time. "The unknown, in general." I shrug. "Those are the biggies."

"I'm really sorry you have all that hanging on you, Ken." Britt sits up straight on the couch. "Almost dying made me a better person, took me outside of myself. Becoming more curious is one of the gifts from my cancer."

"Honestly, that is why I wanted to meet with you," I say. "I am trying to figure out what I believe. And I was hoping to . . ."

Brittany laughs. "Go ahead," she says, sipping her tea. "Ask me anything."

"Well, I feel like all those things I am afraid of, you have dealt with in a big way."

"Jeesh!" She sighs. "I'm not dead yet, Ken!"

"Oh my God, I am so sorry, but—"

"I'm just kidding." She smiles. "I know what you mean. The doctors said that if they hadn't found the cancer when they did, I would have died within two months. So, yes, you've come to the right girl."

"Then can I ask you: How did having cancer change your relationship with God? Like, I don't know, did it make you feel more spiritually connected?"

Britt casts a blank stare out past the balcony. I fear I have asked a question that is hard for her.

I nervously add, "I mean, do you even believe in God?"

"I do," she says sharply. "I was raised Catholic mostly. We would go as a family back in Florida every so often. I did First Communion, but not my Confirmation."

"Same with me," I say.

"Yeah, it wasn't really connecting with me," she recalls. "I remember at some point when I was little someone telling me that being Catholic meant you couldn't have sex before marriage and that God would punish you if you did something wrong, and also God didn't believe in gay marriages and I didn't like that idea. That seemed so judgmental, and I have always been extremely open-minded. Even though I say all that, I still believed in God. Always did. I just didn't know the best way to practice that faith."

"That's also kind of where I am at right now," I say.

"You and probably a lot of people," she says. "It's funny. I remember moving out to L.A. when I was eighteen. I feel that because I am a Pisces I was really hungry to have a deeper connection with God. And getting into show business I felt

I really needed that. If you don't have faith, it is very hard to survive in this business. There is so much that challenges you."

"In what way?" I ask. I think I know what you mean, but . . ."

"First of all, this business can be really hard on your self-esteem. Success can seem completely out of your control all the time, so it helps to believe that somebody else is in ultimate control. For me, it is nice to believe that some higher power has got me covered no matter what. So I had started to really pray and read books and talk to people and basically connect with God, or at least what I knew God to be. And one day a friend gave me a book called *Manifest Your Destiny* by Wayne Dyer."

"Oh, yeah, that's a good book," I say. "I read that a while ago."

"Oh my God, yes," she says. "You should definitely reread it, because it would help you with this journey you are on."

"I've read so many books, Britt," I say. "I've decided that now I need to take more action, to get out of my head and into the world and find my spiritual self through experience."

"Smart. I just mention that Wayne Dyer book because it was life-changing for me for some reason—the idea that you can manifest things that you want or desire. I felt something shift for me spiritually. That was a couple years after *Sweet Valley High*. I was, like, twenty-one or twenty-two. At that point, I would say I was not religious, but spiritual. And I would still describe myself that way."

Brittany stands up and walks toward her balcony. "You wanna get some fresh air?"

"Sure," I say, following her outside.

We lean on the railing of her balcony, watching a flock of seagulls soaring inland as the sun is starting to drop toward the ocean horizon. Brittany's attention is fixed out in the Pacific. She seems much more peaceful than when I had last seen her. The girl I remember then was always running around exercising, hustling, driving around L.A. with her busy life.

"You're different," I say. "It's obvious."

She laughs. "You mean, not as crazy?"

"You're calmer."

Brittany smiles and asks, "Do you meditate, Ken?"

"I have but never too seriously," I reply. "I mean, I've used breathing to calm myself and stuff like that. But I never have been able to stick with it. But I've started doing yoga again recently, mostly to help calm me and get myself to focus on breathing. That is meditation technically, right?"

"Definitely," she says.

"Why did you ask me if I am meditating?"

"Because when I read that book I started to do a little bit of meditating. I did that for a little while and I remember that being really helpful for me. I wasn't taught by a teacher, but learned how to do it in that book. I remember closing my eyes and trying to rest my mind. I was trying to still my thoughts and feelings. Your thoughts and feelings become your reality, and meditation helps you turn off the noise and get in touch with your true self. It helped me and helped my career a lot too."

"Do you still meditate?" I ask.

"Are you kidding?" Brittany arches her eyebrows and stares at me as if I am nuts. "Every day, usually twice a day. Twenty minutes in the morning and twenty in the evening. It is about quieting the mind and releasing a lot of stress. Honestly, I don't think I would be here with you right now if I didn't meditate. It has saved me."

There's a knock on the front door; it's the food-delivery guy.

I head back inside to the couch as Brittany gets the goods and unpacks the veggies and rice she's ordered. She brings me a plate and joins me on the couch.

"So were you meditating when you were diagnosed?" I ask between bites.

"Actually, no," she says. "I was at a place where I was kind of neglecting myself. And maybe that is why it happened."

"Why, what happened?"

"The cancer," Britt answers. "I was so busy with working and feeling like just in a whirlwind. That was my life. With the cancer I felt kind of smacked upside the head. I was spiritually disconnected at that time. I didn't have a real spiritual practice. I wasn't going to a church, wasn't doing yoga or meditating. I would read spiritual books from time to time, but I didn't have a spiritual practice. I was in a relationship and focused more on the guy than on myself. In fact, I was focused on everything outside of myself. I wasn't nourishing my spirit."

"So you feel like God gave you cancer as a sort of . . ."

"A wake-up call," she answers matter-of-factly. "I think I was on a train track and I was rushing really fast in one direction, but I needed to be derailed and put on another train. I feel like God was like, 'You need to slow down and sit down for two years and look at your life.' I needed stillness for a while."

"But didn't you ever have that 'Why me?' kind of moment? Like, 'What did I do to deserve this?'"

Britt pauses. After a few seconds of looking down at the floor in thought, she looks at me and says, "Not really. I didn't go, 'Why is this happening?' I was like, 'OK, I know this is happening for a reason.' On a spiritual level, I was like, I just need to know why, I wanted the lesson to come through to me. I feel like everything happens for a reason and the whole time I just wanted to know what I needed to learn from it."

"So what did you learn?" I ask.

She puts her plate down on the coffee table and settles back cross-legged on the couch. "Oh, gosh, Ken—so many things. First of all, it really showed me the importance of my family and really made clear to me that I definitely want a family. And, um, I think it really showed me how much I need other people, the importance of having connection. I know it might sound so simple, but when you get something like cancer you don't realize how connected we all are. I didn't share my story for so long with people and then I realized I have to reach out to people and needed to connect with other people and reach out. It just made me realize how much I need people. I am sorry I didn't tell you or call you back when I was going through it, but that was part of me being closed off. It might not sound like such a big deal, but I am always like, 'Oh, I can do this on my own.' But you know what I realized? You can't do it on your own. When something like this happens, you need everybody."

She begins to cry. "The cancer was very fast-moving, Ken. I got the MRI results and that very day, the doctors were telling me I had to start chemo the next day. They said that within a couple months, I would die. I needed to treat it right away."

"Wow, I can't imagine what that's like," I say. "You realize you basically lived everyone's worst nightmare."

"But you know what?" she says. "It brought me closer to God."

"How so?" I ask.

"Going through that chemo, knowing that I could die. I went through the darkest, most physical, emotional pain of my life, and that was like the one constant that was with me always: God. You know what I mean?"

"You never felt alone."

"Yeah," she says wiping her tears with a napkin. "I had been stripped of everything. My job, my home, my hair. I moved into my sister's guesthouse and just hunkered down. I was like 130 pounds and dropped to below 100 pounds. Being stripped of everything, of my looks, my health . . . it just . . . brings you closer to the truth. And I feel like that truth is God."

Tears are streaming down her cheeks. I lean over and rub her back. "I'm sorry," I say.

"Don't be," she sniffles. "This is good for me."

I hand her a napkin; she blows her nose. "You know, Britt, what you're sharing with me is so beautiful. You are reminding me of that famous Audrey Hepburn quote right now."

"Which one?" Britt asks.

"Uh, let me Google it," I laugh. I quickly thumb through my iPhone and find the quote I once read attributed to her in a biography about the *Breakfast at Tiffany's* actress, one of Hollywood's most elegant and beautiful stars of all time. I find the alleged Audrey Hepburn quote and read it aloud: "The beauty of a woman is not in a facial mole, but the true beauty in a woman is reflected in her soul."

Britt dabs her eyes. Still crying, she continues, "I know it sounds weird, but, yeah, it was kind of beautiful. There is something about feeling ugly, feeling stripped of that outer shell, that brings everything into focus. Some people would be like, 'Fuck you, God! Why are you doing this to me?' But I didn't feel that way. I wasn't angry at God at all. I just wanted Him to show me what I was supposed to learn. I can deal with all the pain and all the emotional pain. I just needed to know why I was going through this. I would have these conversations with God and say, 'Please just show me what I am supposed to learn here to make this easier,' because that is what was so hard for me."

"I am sorry if this sounds kind of morbid, but did you ever feel like you were going to die, that you weren't going to survive?"

"I definitely had instances when I was going through chemo when I was really sick and thought I would be kicking it out that day. I kept getting really bad infections—in my brain and stuff. My immune system and white blood count got so low that if I got any kind of infection I could just get sick. You can't touch soil and can't be around animals. So it was just during those times that I felt like I could die."

"Were you scared?"

"Not really," she says. "I feel like our souls live on. So I was not scared, but I didn't want to die because I didn't want my twin sister to go through pain and loss, but I just believed that my soul would live on. That is how I feel. I am not afraid of dying. I don't have that fear. I don't have all the answers, but I don't think my soul dies. I think my body dies, but I live on. I don't know what exactly happens, but I am OK with the mystery."

"I'm not," I tell her. "It all freaks me out."

"Aw, Ken. That is your brain freaking out, not your soul. Your soul has all the answers. You just got to turn your brain off."

"So I need to meditate, is what you are saying."

"Yes, because what I learned through the cancer was when everything else—all the noise in my life—was taken away from me, I got closer to God. I started taking Transcendental Meditation classes and doing yoga. In the silence, I not only found great comfort, but it brought me closer to God. That's how it saved me. It got me through the darkest days."

"So did you meditate today?" I ask.

"Yes, I did actually."

"Where?"

"On my floor, sitting against the wall."

"What does it entail?"

"It's hard to explain how it works, but I get comfortable, close my eyes, and slow my breath. Then I go through a whole series of exercises to relax my mind and then I recite my own personal mantra given to me by a guru."

"What's your mantra?" I ask.

Brit laughs. "I can't tell you! It's not supposed to be shared. I repeat it to myself silently."

"OK, sorry," I say, feeling like a total noob.

"It's OK," she says. "You can learn how to do it yourself."

"I've always wanted to get into meditation, but, I don't know, it's hard for me to sit that still for that long, to be honest."

"Meditation will help you still your mind," she says. "It just takes practice."

"But what I am curious about is that, OK, it might relax my mind and center me, but I am trying to find God. How does meditating connect you with God?"

"Look, Ken. I don't pretend to know everything, or have

all the answers. All I can say is that I just feel that the more I can still my mind and not use my mind so much and be present with people and practice that and do it twice a day my mind is less active. And I can just be with you. I feel like God is in all of us. So I am able to be more within myself and not in my mind all the time. When I am meditating it gives me a moment to be open to God. So instead of praying, or talking to God, by meditating I am quieting everything and available to hear things. I feel like I am closer to God because I am quiet and still and able to listen."

The closest person to me who has ever died is my father. It happened on a very cold day in February 1995. Dad had been diagnosed with lung cancer a year earlier at the age of fifty. A few months after he stopped doing chemo while I was working at a newspaper in Virginia, I got the call from my little brother, Kris, who told me, "You better get the fuck home. Dad is unconscious, they rushed him to the hospital."

He died while I was midflight on my way home. That evening, I landed in Buffalo and rushed home to hear what happened from Kris:

> "It all happened so quick, Kenny. I woke up around nine and went upstairs to take a shower and he was sitting in the living room sticking the oxygen tube into his mouth and freaking out. His eyes were popped open real wide. He was all disoriented and didn't know what was going on. He was trying to say things, but it was like he was too out of breath to get the words out. He was speaking like he had just run a mile. I don't know if he was hallucinating or what, but he didn't even know who I was. He kept turning his head and, like, he was seeing people walk by

that weren't there, he would say stuff like, 'Kenny, what are you doing here?' Then it was just gibberish. Nothing made sense. He was done, man. He was on his way out. It was like his organs were shutting down.

"I called the hospice nurse, then I called Kevin and Keith. That's when I called you too, and said, 'You better fly home fast.'

"While I was calling everyone, he got up and walked to the bathroom, still holding the oxygen tube in his mouth, and he sat down to take a shit. He kept moaning and saying he had to take a shit real bad, so I told him to just do it and then go lay down. But he kept saying, 'I can't go, I can't go,' and all of a sudden he stood up and walked back to the living room with his pants around his ankles. I don't even think he realized his pants were down, man. He was just totally out of it.

"It was snowing, and it seemed like it took forever for everyone to get there. He didn't want to go to the hospital. We were trying to talk him into it, but he would just say *no*. When the ambulance came, they gave him a shot of something and it settled him down. They put him on the stretcher and carried him outside. But it was so cold that they couldn't get the legs on the fucking stretcher to collapse. They had frozen stiff. Keith was yelling at the ambulance guy to put a blanket on Dad because he was trembling. Finally they got the stretcher to fold up and started pushing him into the ambulance. The last thing Dad said was 'Nooo!'

"He didn't want to go, Kenny. And I didn't want him to go. But the nurse lady kept saying, 'He has to go. There's no choice.'

"We followed the ambulance to the hospital. We all sat there in his room with him for like an hour. His eyes were opened real wide, but he was barely breathing. His chest would just rise a little. He could hear us, though. When I would talk to him, tell him to hang in there and stuff, he would move his eyes from side to side. He knew what was going on. We agreed with the doctors to let him lay there without any machines, no oxygen mask or anything. It was no use.

"The priest came in a little while later and started reciting some prayers to him. The priest said something like, 'You are forgiven for all your sins, Larry,' and Keith was like, 'What sins? That's bullshit!' The priest calmed Keith down and told us, 'Tell him to go. He is holding on for you. He is waiting for you to tell him to go.' So we told him to go, and he went."

Recalling the day my dad died to Brittany, I still feel the same dread, sadness, and anxiety knowing that my father died in such an inglorious, chaotic way—his bodily functions shutting down, his brain misfiring, and him being so scared to die that he didn't want to go to the hospital, only letting go when he was told to after a fruitless struggle. It was and remains the most tragic day in my life.

Twenty-one years later, three thousand miles away in Marina del Rey, I sit beside my friend Brittany, who faced death with grace, peace, spiritual insight, and acceptance.

"In five years, I will be the same age as my father when he died," I tell her. "I don't want to die like he did. Before I die, I want to know God."

VII

WHAT'S GOOD FOR THE GWYNETH IS GOOD FOR THE GANDER

I do some research into how to start Transcendental Meditation (TM) like Brittany does. I find several other celebrity endorsements of the practice:

> *Nothing has ever opened my eyes like Transcendental Meditation has. It makes me calm and happy and it gives me peace and quiet in what's a pretty chaotic life!*
>
> —HUGH JACKMAN

> *Something about TM, something about having that mantra, it is the only time I have that stillness. It's the only way I have ever been able to sit long enough that I open my eyes and I am sad that it is twenty minutes later. It gives me this peaceful feeling and I just love it so much.*
>
> —ELLEN DEGENERES

I've been doing forty years of TM . . . You know how
your phone has a charger? It's like if you had a charger
for your whole body and mind. That's what TM is.

—JERRY SEINFELD

Like Botox, boob jobs, lip fillers, and the coolest new designer handbags, meditation has recently become a celebrity trend that their fans and followers are waking up to as a result.

The pop singer Katy Perry has said TM "helps me find moments of peace" and TM practitioner actress Cameron Diaz has said in an interview, "You don't have to convince somebody to believe in something. You don't have to get them to understand a different faith or spirituality. TM is helping you tap into something that is already inside of you."

And according to the research, there is science to back up all the personal claims of total body-mind benefits. One scientific study found that practicing TM reduces the level of cortisol (the so-called stress hormone) in your body by 30 percent. And a Stanford University team pored over data and concluded that TM was twice as effective at reducing anxiety as other relaxation and meditation techniques.

The world-renowned Cleveland Clinic has trumpeted its health benefits: "Transcendental Meditation doesn't focus on breathing or chanting, like other forms of meditation. Instead, it encourages a restful state of mind beyond thinking . . . A 2009 study found Transcendental Meditation helped alleviate stress in college students, while another found it helped reduce blood pressure, anxiety, depression and anger."

The more I looked into this, the more apparent it was I needed to meditate. Not wanted. Needed.

I went to www.TM.org and found out it required taking

a one-hour class for four consecutive days and cost $240. My reaction first was (a) I am too busy to commit to four days in a row of doing anything and then (b) That's a lot of money for something I may not even like doing. I decided I needed to do something that I could learn on my own. After doing more research, I find out that there is, of course, an app for meditation—although TM requires one to learn it in person. In fact, there are so many apps (Buddhify, Omvana, Insight Timer, Smiling Mind, Dharma Seed, and so on) that I had no clue which meditation app to download. It was like going to CVS and having twenty different brands of aspirin to choose from.

But my friend and E! colleague Ryan Seacrest once told me he had been using an app called Headspace, which was started by a former Zen Buddhist monk named Andy Puddicomb, and it had been a great tool for him. Ryan is one of the busiest human beings I have ever met, always buzzing around distracted, so if he has had time to meditate, then I should be able to find the time.

The app, which features guided meditations led by Puddicomb utilizing techniques he learned from his years spent in a Zen monastery, also has other celebrity fans, including Jessica Alba, Jared Leto, Gwyneth Paltrow, and Emma Watson. Headspace, perhaps because it is headquartered in L.A.'s hippieville Venice Beach, has the Hollywood stamp of approval more than the others. Perhaps it helps that its motto of being "a gym membership for the mind" is just the kind of easy-to-understand practice Hollywood tends to love.

However, something I must bear in mind is that the phone has become a source of great anxiety for me over the years. It's where I get emails from bosses telling me I did something wrong, where I get angry text messages from my wife when she's upset with me for not doing enough around the house, where my executive producer orders me to get into work early for some breaking news, where I see social media images of friends who seem to be enjoying life a lot more than I am these days. It's also where I currently have 21,345 unread emails in my Outlook inbox alerting me to changes in my show's shooting schedule, about the interview I have to do tomorrow in Calabasas, and the nonstop reports from correspondents with anonymous sources telling *E! News* super important things like the real reason so-and-so is in rehab or why that crazy blond lady had a meltdown last night on *Real Housewives*. In other words, it's filled with the kind of noise and brain garbage I need to be tuning out if I am going to still my mind and not end up having a garbage can for a brain.

So it's a bit ironic that the first place I go to learn how to meditate and get closer to God is to my iPhone.

When I download Headspace on my phone (for free) and find out I can take the thirty-day introductory course (also for free), I decide to put my TM plans on hold and see first how this Zen-inspired meditation works for me.

After wrapping my morning chat show on *E! Online* (Kris Jenner is angry at Caitlyn Jenner!), I return to my office and close the door. As usual just after we wrap, I am feeling agitated, having just performed live for a half hour, and having several more on-air assignments awaiting me in the next few hours. Rather than busy my mind with checking off tasks (call my agent, email my producer, polish the news script, check my Twitter feed) as I normally do, I draw the shades and sit on my couch. I stick my earbuds in and I open the Headspace app.

The meditation program is laid out in five "packs," basically themed series of Andy-led meditations, including Foundation, Sport, Health, Relationships, and Performance. When I click on Foundation, there's a block of text alerting me that I can't "unlock" the rest of the Headspace library until I complete the first of three "foundation" levels, featuring ten sessions of ten minutes in length. Seems logical. Gotta learn to walk before you can run. But how am I going to sit still for ten minutes?

I press on the button for Level 1, which opens up a description of the beginner series: "Start working towards a clearer and calmer mind by learning the basics of meditation and mindfulness."

I hit Play and set my phone down on the couch as Andy tells me in a calm, reassuring British accent to sit comfortably, straight up, with my feet flat on the floor and to gaze "softly" at the floor a few feet in front of me. I guess you don't lie down or sit cross-legged anymore.

He continues in his soft, hypnotic tone, telling me to take in a deep breath and let it out and to "gently" close my eyes, adding, "And just a feeling of the weight of the hands and the arms just resting on the legs . . ."

He pauses and I sit still as I am told. Feeling my feet, in shoes, on the floor. Shit, I should have done this barefoot. I feel my back against the stiff office couch. But I can't break out of my meditation just to take off my shoes, can I? I feel my hands on the top of my thighs and, realizing they are slightly clenched, I relax them. I really should have loosened my tie before starting this.

Andy continues by telling me to bring the focus back to my body and "check in" and note my overall sensation, specifically saying, "whether it is a feeling of heaviness or lightness in the body or stillness or restlessness . . ."

"Restless" is a good word for what I feel. And tense. The muscles around my eyes are tight from trying so hard to keep them closed for an entire *ten minutes!*

Bloodowoop—a text alert. I crack open my left eye and glance down and press the message box open.

Want me to get you a coffee? I'm going.

It's Erin, my fellow E! correspondent.

sure. Iced latte plz

I put the phone back down and close my eyes.

". . . and in your own time starting at the top of the head and just scanning down through the rest of the body from head to toe. Just starting to become more aware of which parts of the body feel comfortable, relaxed, and which parts may be holding a bit of tension or tightness . . ."

I didn't tell Erin I wanted a large. I could just quickly text her . . . *No! Focus* . . .

". . . now if the mind wanders off at any stage just bring it back to those physical sensations as you scan down toward the toes. And as you scan down just starting to become more aware of the underlying mood and emotional quality of the mind . . ."

Ugh, this is hard. I can't focus. This isn't working—at all!

". . . basically just noticing if there are any strong emotions around right now . . ."

My stomach hurts. It always hurts. What did I have for breakfast? A multigrain bagel. Why does it always hurt?

". . . each time you realize the mind has wandered off, no problem. Just gently bringing the attention back again to that breath. . . ."

Ten minutes? It has to be almost over. I can't believe Brittany meditates for twenty minutes—twice a day!

My mind wants me to get up and grab that coffee from Erin. I want to move around and get some work done. And, oh, I am worried about Jackson's hockey game this Sunday against the Ducks. I hope he doesn't play poorly. There's that stomach pinch again . . .

". . . and now just gently bringing the attention back to the body, back to those physical sensations, the contact between body and the chair, feet and the floor, and hands and arms on your legs . . ."

OK, you almost made it. Almost there.

Andy tells me I may now open my eyes.

I open them and close the app, discouraged at my performance. In fact, I feel like an unmitigated disaster and now have more anxiety over being bad at meditating than I did before. A monk, I am not. OK, fine. That was just the first of ten sessions. I will do better next time. I hope.

Now, about that iced latte . . .

Feeling about as far away from a monk as I was before I meditated, I leave my office and walk across the newsroom to see if my coffee has arrived. And as I wind my way through the cubicle farm I realize my stomach doesn't hurt. And most everything around me—the producers talking on the phone, writers pounding away on their keyboards, the online editor women gossiping about some celebrity, the camera crew setting up a shot for me over by the *E! News* logo—that normally seem to be buzzing about at roadrunner speeds are happening much more slowly. Also, my breathing is more steady, relaxed. Perhaps my meditation session wasn't as fruitless as I thought.

"How's your search for God going?" Leah, one of my *E! News* producers, asks me as I get to my desk in the newsroom. By now, I've been talking about my spiritual quest with everyone at work so much they are probably sick of hearing about it.

"Pretty good," I tell her. "Finally started meditating. I've also been going to church. Just trying different experiences and stuff."

"Have you seen a psychic yet?" Leah asks.

"Actually, no," I reply.

Her question throws me. I've never taken psychics very seriously. Sure, I've seen some psychics on TV, like Theresa "The Long Island Medium" Caputo, John Edward, and Tyler Henry. They offer some very impressive insights to seeming strangers off the street, but I've always regarded these psychics as just being very skilled at reading people, not necessarily possessing any supernatural ability to channel the spirit world— certainly not being able to bring me closer to God.

"Well, I know Brad and Angelina's psychic," Leah says. "Her name is Deseret. She's also done readings for Halle Berry. She's the real deal."

"Oh, I don't know," I groan. "I'm trying to explore things that I am seriously interested in or know that I could believe in."

"So you don't believe in psychics?" Leah asks.

"It seems kind of silly," I reply. "I'm sorry."

"Well, have you ever had a reading done?" she presses.

"One time," I say. "When I was going to grad school in New York City, I was walking around the West Village with my girlfriend and she convinced me to go to one of those sidewalk psychics who sits in the window. The lady was like a card reader or something."

"Tarot cards?" Leah asks.

"I think so," I say. "Maybe a palm reader too. I don't really remember."

"Well, I read people's tarot cards," Leah says with a whisper. "I know a lot of people think it's weird, but I really believe in it. What did that lady tell you?"

I mine my memory for a few seconds and then it comes to me. "I remember her in the middle of the reading looking out the window at my girlfriend, who was standing outside on the sidewalk, and the lady said very seriously, "She's not the one. I see darkness."

"And . . . ?"

"A month later, my girlfriend dumped me."

"See!" Leah says. "She probably sensed something."

I counter that maybe it was a lucky guess. Maybe she saw the way my girlfriend was nervously looking at us as she smoked a cigarette. Maybe she just had an intuition. Or, maybe, she really could see the future by tapping into some other spiritual realm.

"OK, Leah." I open my arms wide. "Tell me about Deseret."

Leah says she has known Deseret Tavares for many years and that she is a bona fide celebrity psychic who owns a shop in the Westwood neighborhood of Los Angeles, just a few miles from the *E! News* studio, and suggests I reach out to her. "I wouldn't recommend her to you if I didn't think she was legit," Leah adds. "She's done readings on me and been super spot-on. I would do you myself, but I don't like to do readings on people I know. It's better for someone to do you cold."

I thank Leah and I get back to doing the, um, Lord's work—Justin Bieber has been seen hanging out with his ex Selena Gomez again and it's our lead story "tonight on *E! News*!" as I exclaim with glee in the audio promo for the show.

Ugh.

At lunchtime, I go for a walk in the neighborhood surrounding my office building. It's a sunny spring day. But as I walk I notice that my demeanor does not match the weather. My stomach has started hurting again. It's like the clenching pain you get when you are nervous, only this pain is near constant, as if my body will not relax and is focusing all its stress onto my gut. I try to breathe deep in and out, just like on the meditation app.

Then, in an effort to lighten my mood, I start listening to the *I Am Rapaport* podcast hosted by actor Michael Rapaport. The guy is a total nut but hilarious and always has really funny, brutally honest takes on the pop-culture news of the day. Michael can say what he really thinks, whereas I must always be careful not to come across too heavy-handed because E! is generally celebrity-friendly. But as I listen in order to escape, instead I am distracted and on edge. The distraction is not so much my stomach pain, but rather what is making my stomach ache again: my thoughts.

Thoughts, I am coming to realize, are absolutely what is at the root of my anxiety and distraction and restlessness, something I've learned doing the beginner series of meditations on Headspace for the last week. Sometimes I will find some semblance of peace, even if just for a minute or so of the ten-minute session, like earlier as I was walking in the newsroom. But my anxiety and worry over my health, my finances, my job, my kids, still persists. It comes back. Everything I read about meditation suggests that this is normal, but as you re-wire your brain's circuitry, it will heal itself and former patterns of thought and worry that take you out of the moment will gradually fade as you learn how to breathe and focus on the present.

In the last few meditation sessions, my Headspace "guru" Andy has been teaching what is called "noting" whenever I have a thought or feeling that takes me away from focusing on my breath, by "just noticing if there are any strong emotions around." Andy soothingly says that when an emotion persists, to simply label it either as a "thought" or a "feeling," and, he says, "by asking the question we create a tiny little bit of space" between ourselves and the distracting thought or feeling. In other words, if what's distracting me from focusing on the breath is my sore stomach, I can just mentally note that it is a "feeling," which creates a "headspace" between my true self and this momentary, passing sensation. It's then easier to drop the emotion and move back to the breath, which in turn allows us to be in a more mindful, present state, and, as my friend Brittany pointed out to me, closer to whatever God or force you feel connected to.

Through this "noting" practice, I have noticed my brain is almost constantly filled with the noise of thoughts that are taking me out of the moment and instead sending me into the past or into the future. And the result is that all this time travel is exhausting me! It's raising my stress level, causing me worry and totally making it nearly impossible to enjoy any single moment. Yet, as much as I am practicing going back to the breath when a thought comes up, it is not stopping the thoughts.

And one particularly distracting thought that keeps cropping up is: What will happen to me when I die? In fact, merely asking the question creates a burning sensation in my gut, as if I had swallowed acid. When my mind starts wrestling with the range of answers—such as "I die and turn into soulless, organic matter"—my mood more often than not grows very dark and depressive. I feel totally on edge. The phrase "existential angst" pops into mind, which *Urban Dictionary* so eloquently defines as such: "Existential Angst is the relation to one being aware of the possibility that life lacks meaning, causing an extreme form of anxiety, and a feeling of despair or hopelessness."

Ugh.

A recent study I read found the average male participant had "sexy thoughts" at least nineteen times a day. I can't say the same for myself, because I am more consumed with about that many "morbid thoughts."

I just can't seem to shake it. The other day at a neighbor kid's birthday party at the beach, I told the kid's surfer dad I thought about death "all the time." He sipped beer from his red plastic party cup and pinched a bitter grimace. "Dude, that's not normal." Finally, yesterday I met with my psychiatrist, Dr. Ettikal, the one who prescribed me Xanax a few months back for when I was overwhelmed with anxiety, and who gave me sleeping pills to help me fall—and stay—asleep. I told the doctor I felt like "a dark cloud" was always hanging over me, and that I couldn't turn around my thinking—or turn it off. As my quivering lips motorboated through my explanation, I spotted him glancing at my hands.

"Are you biting your fingers, Ken?" he asked.

I looked down at my hands and saw swollen red cuticles and chomped-down fingernails, flakes of skin flaring off around the edge of my nails.

"Well," I reply, wiggling my fingers, "I think the answer is obvious."

Dr. Ettikal suggested I start taking Prozac, a very reliable drug that treats depression, saying it "might make life a little easier" for me until I can get a better, healthier perspective on my life. I tell him I would rather not add another drug to my system, but I would think about it. I tell him I've been recently trying meditation and seeking spiritual answers to calm and center me.

"How's that working out?" he asks.

"Sometimes it calms me, sometimes it doesn't."

"I suggest you definitely keep on doing that," he says. "But there are some other options I can help you with too. I will write the prescription, but you don't have to fill it. See how things go for you."

As I'm thinking (there I go again, thinking!) about the doctor's suggestion yesterday that I go on more meds, I realize that given what Leah told me about finding comfort in a psychic's perspective, it can't really hurt trying. After all, I am pretty desperate.

So after talking to Leah, I look up Deseret Tavares online, where I find a giant picture of the pretty Colombian and her bio: "Deseret Tavares is a celebrity psychic, life coach, and broadcast personality, known for offering intuitive guidance to a broad roster of celebrity and international clientele. Her predictions have included foresights into the earthquakes in Chili and Haiti, as well as some of Hollywood's most highly-publicized romantic hook-ups and break-ups."

Her site also lists her "abilities" as: "Psychic / Medium / Tarot Reader / Channeler / Energy Healer / Meditation / Chanting / Spell-craft / Paranormal Space Clearing."

Her list of skills seems fairly predictable, except for the last two. There's "Spell-craft." (What is she, a witch?) I look up the definition: "Magical practices involving the casting of spells." OK . . . so she *is* a magician and a witch. Noted. But I am keeping an open mind.

As for her doing "Paranormal Space Clearing," I also have to look up what that means because I truly have no clue. A quick search informs me that it involves the removal of "harmful entities, ghosts, and spirits." Isn't that what they do in *Ghostbusters*?

Normally, I would just laugh and let my logical, analytical mind do its business of closing myself off to mystics and unverifiable spiritual goofiness. But look where being closed off has gotten me. I need to seek answers down any path right now. The worst thing that can happen is that whatever she tells me, or sees in my aura, or whatever ghosts communicate to her, turns out to be a bunch of baloney. I already think it is, so I might as well go through with it. I am reminded of what Adam Carolla said about atheists who claim there is no chance at all God is real: There is no way they would know that.

Despite my reservations, I call Deseret's shop, Mystic's Altar, to set up an appointment, and the man who answers immediately connects me directly with Deseret.

"Hi, Ken!" she shouts through what sounds like a speaker-phone.

"Yep."

"Leah told me you might be calling," she says with a giggle. "So you want to come see me?"

"Yes," I reply. "You come highly recommended."

"I do my best," she says. "Not sure what Leah told you, but I am clairvoyant, and I have all my senses in a spiritual sense activated. I can hear spirits, I can hear guides, they communicate telepathically and I can hear that. I have studied magic abroad for over twenty years and have been learning to channel my energy, my gift. My whole journey brought me to open the store."

"Leah says you've worked with a lot of celebrities," I say. "So you really have worked with Brad and Angelina?"

"Oh, yes," she says. "And it's quite an interesting story, but I will tell you that when we meet."

I hear a clicking sound, like a car's turn signal. "Are you driving? We don't have to talk now."

"Oh, yeah, I am. I am in Glendale and trying to park, honey." Deseret doesn't talk as much as she chirps, with the words rolling off her tongue in a prominent Colombian accent that, at the risk of seeming cliché, is not too unlike Sofía Vergara. "But before I go, honey, what I will say is the interesting thing about the celebrities is that most of them already have this mind-set of being focused on where they are going, and they do believe in themselves. They have the power to manifest things and are strong. A lot of them are spiritual and meditate and practice yoga and eat right. So I do like working with them because many of them are very open and it's easier to access their energy."

"Well, I am looking forward to it," I say. "But, I have to admit, I'm a little nervous."

She laughs. "There's nothing to fear. All I tap into is the truth. And, as they say, the truth will set you free!"

The truth is that I don't feel free at all. I am a prisoner of my general anxiety, existential confusion, and daily distractions that have my mind focused on a thousand things yet nothing at the same time.

VIII

BREATH IS THE
NEW BLACK

Reporting on the frenetic world of Hollywood celebrity only feeds my distraction from myself. A sensational story recently has followed the troubling story of actress Taryn Manning, who has been accused of beating her ex-girlfriend and splashing her with a cleaning solution. Manning stars as a disturbed felon in the Netflix series about a group of women in prison called *Orange Is the New Black*. The accusations against her would suggest Taryn's life is imitating her art: Taryn was arrested for assault.

Throughout my career, I have developed a knack for reaching out to stars in crisis and offering them the opportunity to share their side of the story with a trusted journalist who will play fair and not sensationalize the interview. Reality stars caught in cheating scandals . . . pop stars recovering from addiction who want to explain how much they've changed . . . actors whose careers have been hurt by personal drama. Since Taryn fits firmly in this last category, I tell my boss that I am going to track her down for an interview, starting my search with every journalist's favorite research tool: Google. Within minutes, I learn that the thirty-seven-year-old, who grew up in a trailer park in Arizona, is very active on social media and, in fact, she follows me on Twitter. Maybe she's an E! fan. Encouraged, I follow her back and send her a direct message:

> Hey T. Saw that story. Look, I've forever been a fan but finally saying "hey"... if you ever need help or facts straightened... feel free to hit me up anytime. I'll help. Hope to meet ya—ken

Just a few hours later, Taryn writes back and shares that her ex is trying to "ruin" her even though she is innocent and has done nothing wrong.

I reply:

> After 20 years doing what I do in Hollywood, working in this biz, surviving, I've been through a lot of shit too. I have empathy. Anyway, if you ever just feel like you need a friend in the media don't hesitate. We all need friends, a team; people who won't F you. Talk soon...

Taryn asks for my number, and several days later she calls me. She tells me her side of the story, admits she has been under a lot of stress and wants to clear her name, but her lawyers are advising her to keep her mouth shut. She sounds very upset, her voice cracking with emotion.

"That makes sense," I tell her. "If there is a right time to do an interview, please know I am here."

"Thanks for understanding," Taryn says.

"Of course," I say. "It sounds like it's been a real hard time for you."

"Honestly, Ken, it has." Taryn lets out a long sigh. "Thank God I meditate. It has saved me."

"You meditate?" I reply. "So do I. Well, I have recently started to at least."

"A while ago, I learned Buddhist meditation," she says. "And I have been trying to follow Buddhist practices."

I tell her I recently have begun meditating with the help of a former Buddhist monk on the Headspace app.

"That's cool, Ken," she says. "I have found solitude by meditating. It has taken the pain out of my head. The truth is that it's been a real hard time, and I have even thought about quitting acting because this tabloid part of the business is so shitty. But every time I meditate, I focus on love—onto myself, and I send it out. It really works. My heart is fully opened and blossomed and bleeding, Ken."

"Thank you for sharing all this with me," I tell her, explaining how I am amid my own search for God and peace and spiritual meaning in my life and I have been trying to be open to new beliefs and practices.

"I believe in God," Taryn says. "I was raised in the Bahá'í Faith and was taught that there is unity in all religions and our purpose is to love God and in so doing love ourselves."

Taryn doesn't sound like the whack-job actress that "Page Six" gossip items have made her out to be. Of course, I learned long ago not to believe everything you read. Yet clearly she has made some poor choices in her life. But haven't we all? I wish Pastor Brad's "No Perfect People Allowed" slogan was painted over the Hollywood sign. Then, perhaps, the veil of perfection that cloaks the celebrity world would be lifted, thus freeing the masses from the unattainable Hollywood standards of beauty and lifestyle and money.

Even so, I am surprisingly impressed with Taryn's spiritual awareness and her ability to articulate it with a relative stranger with such vulnerability and openness.

"I know I wanted to talk to you about doing an interview," I tell her. "But to be honest, what you just shared with me is, personally speaking, exactly what I needed to hear. But if you ever need to share anything in the media, I am here for you. I don't really ever take sides when I am reporting on a story. I am on the side of the truth."

Taryn doesn't reply. I hate awkward silences, especially over the phone.

I quickly add, "So there you have it."

"Just keep meditating, Ken," Taryn says. "That's where you will always find truth."

IX

KEEP UP WITH THE KARDASHIANS

Today is Easter, the one Sunday every spring when most Christians worldwide celebrate the resurrection of Jesus Christ three days after he was crucified, as told in the epic that is the New Testament. Lately, I have been reading the Bible, particularly the Gospels, for the first time in my life with a spiritual focus. And somewhat to my pleasant surprise, I am experiencing the Bible as a great resource for life lessons and spiritual growth. The stories about overcoming hardship, of allowing faith in a higher power to guide your heart, of the power of love for one another, bleeds through so many of the chapters and the characters in them. I have even had fun reading the books by the apostles Matthew, Mark, Luke, and John to compare their accounts of Jesus. I will never be a biblical scholar, but my reading has deepened my understanding of one of the world's most significant historical figures.

While reading the other day, I stumbled upon a verse that stands out for my searching self in Hebrews 11:1: "Now faith is confidence in what we hope for and assurance about what we do not see." The quote stopped me, and I reread it many times, aloud to myself. Historically, faith has been my barrier to believing in any one religion's version of God. To me, faith has always meant suspending disbelief in order to have a belief. That is, faith is, according to Merriam-Webster's dictionary, a "firm belief in something for which there is no proof." My problem is why would God give me a mind so capable and inclined to question everything unless there is compelling evidence, but then require me to turn off my God-given cerebral instinct in order to believe in *Him*? That simply doesn't seem logical! But as I read that chapter in Hebrews, about how faith in God has helped people throughout history avoid temptations, helped them endure persecutions, and allowed them to achieve a grace in the face of enormous terrors, dangers, and injustices, I realize that it's not just about "having faith" but rather about "having faith in the idea of faith." Hebrews 11:1 describes faith as being about having the confidence to get your ego brain out of the way in order to allow a power greater than we can see into our lives. Under this definition, the foundation of the Christian notion of faith is not too unlike that of Buddhism, Hinduism, and even the yoga practices associated with them in which turning off the self is what ultimately allows one to find their true self. I found a beauty to the message that I had never quite grasped.

And on this Easter Sunday, I find myself grappling with whether I can take that leap with Christianity—or any religion, for that matter. So while today is considered the high point of the Christian worship calendar, I don't feel as if, personally, I'm at my spiritual high point. I'm definitely not at my low; I'm closer to believing in . . . something.

In my quest to believe in something, I've been making the

hour-long drive to Kris Jenner's church most every Sunday to
be inspired by Pastor Brad Johnson's always-relatable sermons.
I spot Kris and her boyfriend, Corey, seated in the front row
when I walk into the sanctuary of the California Community
Church a few minutes late for the 9:30 a.m. service. Kris is
wearing a black-and-white pantsuit, her famously cut-short
black hair perfectly sculpted. The band has already begun
playing, so I shake Corey's hand and give Kris a quick hug
before settling into the chair to Kris's left.

I notice that all the chairs in the front row have Reserved
placards on them. This isn't normal. Usually all the chairs are
open to anyone, though Kris usually likes to sit in the front
row right below Brad's lectern.

"Who are these seats reserved for?" I whisper to Kris.

"Supposedly, the rest of the family," she says with a shake
of her head, checking the time on her iPhone. "If they ever
freakin' show up."

Moments later, Khloe Kardashian, looking Kentucky Derby–
ready in an all-white pantsuit and topped with a matching white
hat, scurries self-consciously into a seat a few down to my left.
I glance behind her and can see through the front window an
armada of paparazzi flashing their cameras in the parking lot.
Then, behind Khloe I see a very tall black man in a gray hooded
sweatshirt and brown-tinted sunglasses clutching a Starbucks
cup. He squeezes between the narrow aisle leading to the front
row. It's her husband, Lamar Odom.

I crane my neck back at the packed church and notice pretty
much all eyes are on Lamar. Not just because he is nearly seven
feet tall. Not just because he is a former L.A. Laker. Not just
because he hasn't been to this church in over two years. The
biggest reason why the congregation is focused on Lamar is

because it is one of his first public appearances since he almost died several months ago after overdosing.

I watch as he plops his bony frame into the seat beside Khloe. She has nursed him to health ever since he lay in a coma in that Vegas hospital, outside which I stood for days reporting on his overdose, and where I prayed for him at the request of a family member and where, much to my surprise, he woke up as if prayers had been answered.

That moment was the catalyst that spurred my desire to reconnect with my spirituality, to get to know this God from whom I asked for help and used to speak to regularly. It led me to attend Bible study, to talk to spiritually minded people I've met through work, to start meditating, to pray again, to start coming to this church with Kris Jenner, and to appreciate the Bible for the first time as an adult.

As the band jams its folk rock, I stand up and, crouching down, step over to Khloe and give her a hug and an air-kiss. I lean over and shake Lamar's hand.

"Happy Easter, my friend," I say.

"Thank you, Ken," he replies in a mumble. "Good to see you, my man."

This moment easily could never have happened. By all accounts, Lamar not only could have never come out of that coma, but he could have been permanently brain damaged and unable to walk again. At the time I remember hearing a report that he would be in diapers the rest of his life. Tabloids claimed if he lived he would be "a vegetable."

But months later, here he is in a church with me, fully functional, both of us here to acknowledge that there is a force greater than us that just might be capable of performing miracles.

As the band stops and Pastor Brad steps up to the pulpit, Kourtney Kardashian, carrying her infant son, rushes to the front with her blue-jean-clad supermodel sister, Kendall, who sits to my immediate left and rubs my shoulder with a friendly hello. I remember when Kendall was eleven and I would see her run up the stairs when I showed up to the family house, a shy kid. Now she is nineteen and one of the most famous models in the world. Kendall fiddles on her phone and checks her Instagram as Pastor Brad broadcasts his welcoming smile to the congregation.

But sitting here with members of arguably the most famous family in the world, I am reminded that at the end of the day we are all human and, no matter how famous or rich or gorgeous, there is a humility to being human that is revealed when we all sit and worship a God we hope is listening. In the old days, not everyone owned a Bible, or had the Internet, so gathering with others in a church to get preached to was practical. These days, it is a choice to congregate in a group and proclaim your faith . . . or, in my case, seek to know it. There is a beauty in it that transcends Kendall's physical beauty. A church service honoring a figure who is believed to have died for our sins reveals a beauty of human truth—not a skin-deep beauty of falsity. As unsure as I am about the validity of the historical Jesus's significance, I am glad I came, because I feel as if I have purpose.

Brad begins his energetic Easter sermon, reminding us that today is the day we celebrate the resurrection of Jesus Christ, reading from John 11:25: "I am the resurrection and the life. The one who believes in me will live even though they die."

Brad says, "Resurrection is when something has died and come back to life," sharing that he has gone through times he had failed and felt spiritually dead but his faith brought him back to life. The preacher, disgraced and suicidal just a few years ago, is a compelling messenger.

Brad continues, "There are people in the room who are addicts." Brad doesn't glance at Lamar, but I sense that he has specifically mentioned addicts to get his attention. I sneak a peek at Lamar, who stares up at Brad with full attention as Brad adds, "And you know there was a time when people wrote you off, hopeless. And now you're sober. God specializes in resurrection."

Brad goes on to tell the story of Lazarus, whom Jesus brought back from the dead, after his sister asked for Jesus's help. "God will give you whatever you ask," Brad reads from John 11:22, before closing his Bible and addressing the congregation. "This Easter Sunday could be your moment. Your faith could rise and you can believe that with God all things are possible. . . . Some of you feel like there is a boulder sitting on your chest and you don't have the strength to roll the stone away. . . . On Easter, I want you to remember that God rolls stones away. He did it for Lazarus, he did it for himself, and he will do it for you."

At the heart of Christianity is this very uplifting, hopeful message. Yet so much of that inspiration seems to be lost in the politics of faith these days. Some Christians, certainly not all, are still waving their Bibles in judgment at gays, nonbelievers, people they deem to be godless or heathen for not following their God. But when you strip that all away, and read the words in the Bible, the foundational message is an inspiring, uplifting, and hopeful one: We can have eternal spiritual life with faith in Jesus Christ. It's that message of hope that has kept me coming back to this church.

I glance over at Lamar, who sits expressionless as he soaks in Brad's closing prayer.

"It is a personal decision to become a follower of Jesus," Brad says as the keyboard player chimes in softly in the background. "I am not talking about understanding it intellectually; I am talking about personalizing it in your heart. Jesus went to the cross for you, for your sins, and he rose from the dead so you can be forgiven. The same voice that called Lazarus from the grave calls you out of your sins today. . . . He loves you and forgives you and he makes you brand-new. You can't do that for yourself."

Brad then asks everyone who wants to know Jesus in their heart to pray with him: "Heavenly Father, forgive me of my sins and make me brand-new. I believe you died for me and you rose so that I could be forgiven. Fill me with your spirit so that I can follow you for the rest of my life."

I close my eyes and listen, but I don't recite the prayer with Brad. I love the message, but I don't know whether I believe Jesus is the only way, and especially don't think I agree with Brad that I cannot make myself brand-new, that only Jesus can do that. But I am not sure. That's why, as I hug the Kardashian clan and make plans to see them soon, I still have a lot to figure out about what I believe and don't believe.

One thing I do believe is that whether Lamar showing up to church with me today was an act of God or just a coincidence, his very existence gives me hope that no matter how low or how lost I may feel, I still believe in the values of hope, faith, and love.

I step toward Lamar to say goodbye and notice a tattoo on his inner left hand. It's the cursive initials "KO" for Khloe

Odom, his long-suffering wife who has just nursed him back to health from his stroke.

Then I have a revelation: I may not be ready to commit my soul to Jesus Christ, but I am prepared to commit my body to three values I hold dear.

A few days later, it's my forty-sixth birthday. I wake at six o'clock, pour coffee into a to-go mug, and begin my hour-long commute from Hermosa Beach by crawling up La Brea Avenue into the E! studios in Hollywood, where I start my fast-paced typical morning—a quick stop in the makeup room to get made pretty by Liz, head to wardrobe and put on the shirt and tie and skinny jeans my stylist has hung up for me, hustle upstairs to the newsroom for the morning meeting with our executive producer, and then walk up to our third-floor studio and get in place at the table for our daily web show *Live from E!* On the air, we talk about how it's Kourtney Kardashian's birthday and discuss her most recent Instagram post. I don't mention that Kourtney and I share the same birthday—April 18—but after we wrap I do text Kourtney, a friend, as I have for many years on this date.

happy bday, kourt! Hope you have a great one!

u too ken. Make it special!

I plan to.

After recording some voice-over promos for tonight's *E! News*, I head to my office and probe the web, researching different designs that symbolize faith, hope, and love. One site features an image and describes its meaning as such:

Love is a supreme motivator. Faith in God can cause miracles. And hope is what keeps us going even in difficult situations. Sometimes just seeing a faith hope love tattoo on a passerby can bring about a positive change in the viewer. These three words are not mere spellings. They are deep concepts that can change the world. They bring about a positive feeling in a person. This positivity will then manifest into an inner strength that makes life easier. Problems don't seem insurmountable anymore. Faith, love and hope are the pillars on which a good and peaceful life rests.

Now I know what will be my birthday present to myself. I print out the image and when we wrap the show shortly before five, I drive north a few miles to Kat Von D's tattoo parlor in Hollywood.

"Make yourself comfortable," my tattoo artist, Mikey, tells me, patting the table. He points at it as if I'm a dog and he is my master. "Don't be shy, now."

I strain a smile and hop up on the bench, gently easing onto my back.

My stomach grinds like a cement mixer as I lick my dry lips and fold my hands across my chest. A pocket of air sits locked in my tight lungs, and pressing my palms down on my breastbone, I grunt it out, the exhale sounding like a hockey puck scraping through a cheese grater.

For much of the past year, especially before I began praying and meditating, this basic biological function—breathing—has not been an easy thing for me to do. And Mikey's not at all helping me relax when he looks down and asks with a snaggletooth grin, "So this really is your first time?"

"Yeah," I reply. "Definitely."

"Well, you're in good hands."

I stare at the ceiling in a corpse pose. This position reminds me of when I get my annual MRI checkup, when my nearly six-foot-long body is inserted into a white tube and injected with a dark-colored dye that spreads through my arteries to bring contrast to the image of my brain. For close to an hour, with my head rendered all but immovable in a cage, my skull is scanned to find whether the tumor near the base of my brain, first discovered nearly twenty years ago and (mostly) removed by a surgeon, has grown back. Obviously, these exams aren't exactly a chill vibe. In fact, they freak me out. My anxiety was made worse a few years ago when the MRI report came back with this finding: The tumor, which had been dormant since the late 1990s, had spread, requiring me to up my medication and hope it didn't spread throughout my brain . . . and kill me.

This probably explains why most any lie-down-with-my-face-up procedures—be it a dental exam, a massage, donating blood—can bring on the Monster. Who's that? He's the flood of anxiety, breathless panic, the sense of dread that breaks into my skull and hijacks my brain, holding me prisoner until the "anxiety attack" subsides. Over the years, I have tried to manage the Monster. I've done hypnotherapy, gone into $200-an-hour talk therapy where I was diagnosed with PTSD, and I even tried a controversial treatment used on war-torn soldiers. It is called EMDR, which stands for eye movement desensitization and reprocessing, in which I recall my traumatic events while the psychiatrist gets me to focus on a moving light that gets my gaze moving laterally. It was supposed to detach pain from the memory. It didn't work. I resorted to taking the occasional Xanax to make it stop, though it's like putting a Band-Aid on an ax wound.

Unlike an MRI exam, the session I have scheduled with Mikey isn't necessarily something I must do to stay alive. In fact, a Google search I conducted earlier today at my desk in the *E! News* room uncovered a host of reasons—from infections to hepatitis to nasty allergic reactions—that is evidence that what Mikey is about to do to me is perhaps not only unhealthy but potentially lethal (albeit small risk of that). The inherent risks didn't stop me, however, from leaving work and driving straight to this building just off Hollywood Boulevard.

Here I lie
Not to die
But to seek some grace
I want to escape my inner rat race

Mikey slides his fingers into black latex gloves, takes hold of my left arm, and extends it straight out to the side like an arm of Jesus on the cross.

"Don't move," he says. "Got it?"

"Uh-huh."

Some of my unease may come from the fact that I just met Mikey for the first time about an hour ago and know nothing about him other than what I read on the web, which, quite frankly, wasn't very reassuring. OK, fine. His page actually had no bio on it whatsoever; instead, just a photo of Mikey in a black T-shirt with "666" printed on the front in demonic lettering. In the pic, I could see a sleeve of tattoos coating his right arm, which was cocked at the elbow so he could flash the satanic devil-horn sign with his pinky and forefinger. A metal ring dangled from between his nostrils. Yet, still, I came here. I am that desperate.

Now I am beneath that very same dark-haired man in this box of mirrors and rock music blaring, with lots of nervousness, excitement, and an intention to make this the kind of spiritual experience that I could really use on this day, my forty-sixth birthday.

"Shouldn't you strap me down or something?" I ask him with an unconvincing half smile. "You know, like, just in case I move?"

He looks away and laughs with a machine-gun patter, his thick black earrings dancing with his overstretched earlobes.

"Nah." He picks up the needle. "You can do it. I have faith in you."

Faith: That's what I've been seeking, yearning for, needing, but have not yet found. The spiritual equivalent of glasses—something, anything—to help me see my true self.

I've been thinking more about death all the time. In the car on the freeway. In bed with my kids. Sitting in front of the camera at work. Actually, I think about death so much it makes it hard to focus on life. I often think about how short life is, how the kids are growing up so fast and how my body aches more often and in more places. And twice a week, when I must swallow the Tic Tac–shaped pills to keep the tumor from growing in my head, I think about death.

No longer having any defined spiritual belief system framing the Big Picture for me makes the specter of death the most anxiety-inducing thought I have these days.

So, at forty-six, this is where I stand: Half a lifetime ago, I thought I pretty much knew everything. Now that I realize I don't know what I believe, it's as if I know nothing.

Lost (adj.)—not knowing where you are or how to get to where you want to go

"How long will this take?" I ask Mikey.

Mikey rubs an antiseptic wipe on the veiny spot just below the crease of my inner arm. It's the same place from which blood has been drawn, where drugs have been injected, and, now, the place where I can look for the comfort I seek with a permanent stamp defining me.

"Like a half an hour—tops," he answers. "Why? You in a hurry or something?"

"Not at all," I say. "Just curious."

I shut up. I don't want to rush him. A micro-slip of his hand would scar my body for life.

I've already acquired plenty of physical and emotional scars—totems to a lifetime of sweet victories and profound disappointments, successes and failures, great beauty and distressing ugliness, of enjoying my health and battling disease, of falling in love and, also, of having my heart shattered in pieces that I still haven't put back together.

Oh, how I wish to feel whole
To escape this hole
I look above
I want love

In the past year or so, my physical pains have become more acute:

- The flare-ups of arthritis in my right hip, from an old hockey injury, cause me to limp and hobble after sitting for long stretches.
- The omnipresent stomachaches; my gut wrings itself into a twist near constantly, from the moment I wake up until I crash into bed, every day for so many months I've stopped counting.
- The sore muscles radiating across my chest and my armpits.
- The pinching pain in my lower neck, the result of my constant staring down at my phone coupled with the poor posture of my two hours on the freeway each day to take me to the E! Studios in Hollywood, where the increasing visits from the Monster have made it harder to focus on my on-camera job that demands a lot of my attention.

I am too young to feel this way. I have too much life ahead of me to have angst and worry and spiritual hollowness cramping my physical self. I keep wondering, Who am I? Why am I here? What is my purpose? What is the meaning of it all?

I've hurt enough in this life to know I don't like pain, thus I've expended a lot of energy avoiding it. I've been burned and I don't want to touch that stove, don't want to tell my wife, Brooke, my true feelings about how at times I feel trapped in this so-called Perfect Life as the clock ticks down to death. So I avoid the pain of an argument (*Just be grateful . . . Stop making yourself crazy with worry*), maybe pop a Xanax to numb myself to the accumulated pain that has come from ignoring the chorus of voices that torture me with songs of warning that I've been disconnected from my true self, from my soul. But how do I find it?

As I watch Mikey towel my arm dry, I remember something I once heard Deepak Chopra say: *In order to heal pain, we must first experience pain.*

With this logic, I suppose I am healing. But I don't like that pain has become my new normal: My guts aching with every step into the unknown through my search for faith, hope, and love in Hollywood.

I've been struggling to find meaning amid the demanding chaos of juggling my role as dad, husband, son, friend, author, and journalist, while also trying to keep a sense of my *unlabeled* self—that is, my true self, the inner self, the soul that gradually has been obscured in the fog of my life chasing celebrities, wheezing in freeway smog, hustling kids to hockey practices and games across the country . . . popping pills to keep the Monster at bay.

> *Something's gotta change today*
> *I say*
> *Or I will feel more sorrow*
> *I need a better tomorrow*

If I'm going to get from Mikey what I want tonight, it'll take sacrifice. That's usually how it works. Though I was one class short of being a religion minor in college, I'm not a religious scholar by any stretch of the definition. But as a seeker I have read at least enough to have passing knowledge of the teachings of Jesus, Buddha, Allah—most of the great spiritual messengers of the world's religions. I've found that they share, among many other similarities, this common message: *You've got to give up something in order to get something bigger.*

And that's been a theme of my life. Move away from home

as a teen to live my college hockey dreams. Go into oodles of graduate school debt to get ahead in journalism. Quit my job as a newspaper reporter in Virginia and drive across the country, with no guarantee of work, to set up shop in Los Angeles to try to make it in the global epicenter of entertainment media.

My move west occurred twenty years ago, back when my celebrity crush was Jennifer Aniston (still is, by the way) and I knew one person in all of Los Angeles (my buddy Glenn). Although I wish I could say the time has flown, it really hasn't. Some periods dragged on as I struggled to keep my career alive and my marriage intact as my life evolved from a private one to that of a marginally famous pseudo-celebrity—that is, I became micro-famous for covering actually famous people. But the Miami Beach magazine parties, the exclusive interviews, the nationwide book tours, tropical vacations with the kids, and their hockey trips across North America did fly by, because this is when I was indeed having fun, connected to my true self. And those moments flew way too fast. In fact, my life has seemed to be moving so quickly I feel as though I can't catch my breath.

Maybe the pain this guy with a tattoo on his forehead and the bottom pierced lip is about to inflict on me will somehow focus my search for meaning, perhaps even bring me closer to God. Maybe the symbol he's about to ink into my arm will be a permanent reminder of what matters most. And maybe this ritual will mark the start of me taking back control of my body, mind, and lost spirit.

Bzzzz.

The instant his needle pierces the soft skin of my inner forearm, I cringe.

Heart racing. Chest tightening. Sweating. *Oh, shit. The Monster!*

I grunt a spray of spit across my lips and look away, catching the pathetic image of myself in the mirror across the room. *What the hell are you doing? Have you lost your mind?*

Soon, I will learn that losing my mind is the very thing I must do before I will find what I'm looking for.

Here I lie
Not to die
But to seek some grace
I want to escape my inner rat race

I lie on the padded bench, frozen in position as Mikey's buzzing needle injects black ink into the pale skin of my left forearm. It's my first tattoo, and also the first time I have ever felt so strongly about something that I would mark it on my body with the symbols of a cross for faith, an anchor for hope, and a heart for love.

Enduring the pain of a dye-injecting needle in order to enjoy this meaningful symbol is a metaphor for all the hardship and struggle I've experienced that has led me to this spiritual journey, that has made me the seeker I am today.

And for the first time since I began my quest late last year in that Vegas hotel room, I feel a renewed sense of spiritual focus, peace, and purpose. Happy birthday, to me.

X

WHO YOU GONNA CALL? BRANGELINA'S GHOSTBUSTER!

I leave work in Hollywood and drive toward the ocean to the corner of Westwood and Olympic, just south of the UCLA campus, where Deseret Tavares's psychic storefront sits wedged between a tailor shop and an antique store.

To kill time, I stroll the cramped gift shop that fronts Deseret's reading room. The shop reeks of incense and scented candles, and shelves are filled with hundred-dollar crystals and various polished stones and gems that allegedly have "mystical" properties. There are books on Wicca and magic and psychic channeling. I find a shelf filled with "aura sprays" for every intended mood, including "Creativity & Flow," "Divine Love," and "Healing and Transformation." It would all spook me out if it didn't all seem so silly.

What the hell am I doing here? I mean . . .

✓ Church—totally conventional place to find God.
✓ Bible study—an earnest, informative pursuit.
✓ Exploring atheism—intellectually mandatory.

✓ Interviewing an actress about her near-death experience—spiritually enriching.

✓ Meditation—a wise, mindful practice.

✓ Tattoo-branding ceremony—a symbolic commitment to my spiritual values.

But coming to a self-proclaimed "witch" to have my cards and palms read as she channels ghosts is, for someone as analytical as me, firmly out of my comfort zone.

What if she tells me I am going to die tomorrow? What will happen if she casts a spell on me? What if I waste an hour being fed a basket of baloney?

Shortly after six o'clock, Deseret emerges from behind the cashier's counter in slacks and a loose-fitting black blouse. "Come on back," she says, gesturing to her office.

I shake her hand. It is soft and lotioned as beaded bracelets shake from her wrist. As I step inside the dark office, Deseret, a middle-aged brunette, closes the door and I take a seat on the other side of her solid wood desk that is littered with crystals and a stack of tarot cards.

"Have you ever been to India?" she asks.

"No."

"You have to," she says. "I have been many times. It's where I've gotten a lot of the artifacts here. It is believed that Varanavata by the Ganges is the oldest city in the world. It was already the oldest city when Jesus walked the Earth. It is a very sacred place with over 2,200 temples all over the city. You see spirituality in every aspect of life. The streets are no wider than two people to walk side by side and you will see people chanting and meditating. In the Ganges they have ceremonies at sunrise and sundown and they clear the energy. They believe once you are buried or burned on the river your soul doesn't return."

"I have heard that," I say. "But to be honest, I have always wondered why I need to go to some special geographic location to have a spiritual experience. One of the most profound spiritual experiences I ever had in my life came in a minor pro-hockey arena in Bakersfield in front of five thousand people. My current search is taking place in Hollywood. If it is about connecting with our souls, why does geography matter?"

Deseret sits with her hands folded on the desk, sitting rigid and listening to me. She cracks a smile. "Good question, Mr. Baker," she says in a Colombian accent. "Because every place has a vibration and a hidden lesson for you. When you go on a spirit quest like you are on, you will go to different places and learn different things that all will teach a lesson."

I arch my eyebrows and nod. That certainly has been the case for me so far, I tell her.

"I have had spiritual experiences in a church, in my living room, in my car and in places like India, Brazil, and Europe. You will find the same thing is true as you go on your journey of faith, I am sure of it."

Deseret is much more articulate and intelligent than I had expected to find from a woman reading tarot cards in an office behind a shop hawking $22 aura sprays.

"As I told you on the phone, I am not very familiar with psychics," I say. "What exactly is your gift and what can you help me with?"

"I use all six senses of the spiritual aspect. You use your eyes to see the physical aspect. But I can use my third eye—

the spiritual aspect of your sight—to see different beings and places and communicate with them. I can travel from one dimension to another and communicate to beings not in this realm. We all can do this. The third eye allows you out of the box we live in. I can hear thoughts and messages telepathically. That allows me to communicate with my spirit guide to get answers. They live on spiritual realms and give you messages. They are similar to voices you hear inside your head that tell you maybe to wear your seat belt or don't go to that meeting. It is a being that walks with you. They are teachers."

"So are these like guardian angels?" I ask.

"The Church would call them that," she says. "Some would call it the Holy Ghost. It is a guide assisting to help you through this. He walks with you and only you. Mine is different than yours."

"So can I have a faith in your spirit world and believe in a spirit guide and be a Christian? I was raised Catholic and this kind of communication was shunned as the work of the devil."

"This is true," she says. "I was born Mormon and Catholic. I went to a Catholic church because in Colombia, where I was born, it was mandatory. I would go to church and the religious school and then head to the Mormon church where my father was a bishop. I had many different experiences. I would know things that others didn't know. I would know passwords and things that were gonna happen or had happened. They thought I was a weird little kid who heard voices. I would say, 'Don't you hear the voice?' They thought I was crazy."

"Did you ever see a psychologist?"

"Yes, I did, and I thought something was wrong with me because I heard voices. They thought I was schizophrenic. But I wasn't. It was very real. If my dad locked my bike I would hear the password to my bike and open it. He would say, 'How did you open it?' I'd say, 'Well I heard the number.' He'd be like, 'How?' I would just say, 'I just heard it and followed the instructions.'"

"Who would tell you?"

"My spirit guide," she says. "It is male. I have seen him and it is definitely a guy."

"What does he look like?"

"He is very, very tall. He is dressed in a long gown down to the floor and has a turban that covers the side of his face. Like what Jesus used to wear, but a lot more slender and you can see his face. Every time I meditate and ask for him to show up, this is what he looks like and this is what shows up."

As I am trying to process that the cute lady across from me has superhuman powers to talk to dead people, Deseret explains that it wasn't until she was out of high school and took a channeling class that she learned she was a psychic medium and began giving readings to people, which eventually led to her gaining a celebrity following after moving to Los Angeles.

"Please don't take this the wrong way, but what do all those oils and incense and sprays have to do with everything you just told me?"

"Everything on the planet has an energy pattern—from a rock to a bug to water. Everything has an energy source. When you work with oils you are working with the essence and energy of a plant. An essential oil in pure form is the pure extract from a plant, is the most powerful form of the plant. It is fifty thousand times stronger. Plants have a spirit. In the plant form, we call those elementals. You develop a relationship with the spirit that lives in the plant and you ask the elemental to help you out. Almost like talking to a spirit."

I ask her about the large crystal and bottle of oil on the desk between us.

"This is amethyst and is a rutile crystal," she says, holding it up in front of me. When I reach for it, she pulls it back. "No, no, no," she says with a smile. "This is my crystal; for you to touch it would diminish its power. This kind of crystal is very special. It helps facilitate the chakras to the spiritual realm."

I apologize to her. I feel like I have broken a psychic rule. But Deseret doesn't seem too concerned and lifts up the tiny bottle.

"This is a potion that helps me channel and read when I want to be more open," she explains. "It opens up my chakra. It is a mixture of different oils and herbs and you charge it with Reiki energy, the crystals are generators. They generate a certain energy, it transforms negative energy into love and also helps you with intuition."

"Honestly, I have told people I was coming and they warned me it was bad luck to see a psychic. They believe you can influence people and push them in a direction. A lot of people have fear about this stuff."

"When you walk into a place like this and your heart or stomach aches you shouldn't walk in. Your spirit will tell you if it is the right place for you. Do you feel comfortable here?"

"Yeah, actually. I do."

"Good," she says with a grin. "You should. I am not one of those fake psychics. That is why I have a following."

"How *did* you get to the point where you are now a celebrity psychic?"

"I had an out-of-body experience for three days at home, after watching a Depeche Mode video."

I giggle. I think she is making a joke. But she isn't.

"I am serious," she says. "I was home in my apartment with my friend Amanda and she loves Depeche Mode. She had a video and I said I am going to sit down and watch the video with her, and we had a couple of glasses of wine and started watching the video. I realize in the video there is a dark spot, and that the dot started to get bigger and bigger and bigger and bigger! It got to the point where it was hypnotizing. It was really strange, and I hear my guide saying to follow the dot. I told my friend and she said I was crazy, she said I am tripping and asked what did I take. I tell her I had some wine and that's it. She's like, 'You're tripping.' But I wasn't. It was like a portal. It was like I was being hypnotized and I am traveling and I can't feel my body.

"My guide comes in and it was the first time I had channeled. My guide starts to tell me the history of the universe and I am telling Amanda to record this, what I am saying, because I probably won't remember. And he begins to tell me the history of the universe, how it was created and what I am supposed to do.

"He showed me a graph. He said that in the beginning it was all darkness. One speck of light, which is God, and the energy started to shift. And that dot was a nucleon, and from that nucleon came different little balls of energy that were born and eventually those balls of energy made this big piece of light and as we became our own gods that light produced different forms of light and eventually made the light bigger. I was like, 'This is really strange; I don't get it.' I'm telling her all this and I was using this terminology that I never use and felt the spirit coming in and out of me, and she is like, 'Why are you speaking weird?' Even my voice sounded different.

"This was over three days."

"You were in this state for three days? Did you sleep?"

"No! It was just in-and-out talking. I kept going in and out of this tunnel and seeing more things. I hadn't talked to my mom in a while and I told my mom what was happening and she is like, 'You've got to turn around. You've got to get out of the tunnel.' So after three days, I turned around and came back and realized that this was my gift. I need to channel this spirit and help other people tap into their spiritual realm. And it just grew from there."

"Depeche Mode did all this? That is so random."

"I know, right? Apparently there is a vibration with the way that they play their music. It emits a vibration that opens up a portal."

"What song was it?"

"It was a whole video! Like a DVD. It changed everything. Soon, I would do readings for people and blow them away with what I knew. Then I began doing them on local TV and I guess I just became known as a celebrity psychic. It just sort of happened. I didn't really plan it that way."

"So who are some of the celebrities you've worked with?"

"Well, my database is huge. I have done probably every regional Latin singer that has come through L.A. I have read Alejandro Fernandez, Jenny Herrera and her brother Gus Herrera. I used to be his personal psychic. In Hollywood, I have done Natalie Imbruglia, Halle Berry, and, as you already know, Brad Pitt and Angelina Jolie."

"You did them separate or together?"

"I did them together. This was a couple of years back. Brad gave a reading from me to Angelina as a birthday present."

"They just showed up one day?"

"No." She laughs. "Their assistant called the shop and says,

'Would you do a reading in a limo?' I was like, 'Sure, I guess.'
She said, 'OK, they are going to come and pick you up.' I
didn't ask any questions. She gave me her name, but didn't say
who it was for. The limo driver was late and kept calling and
saying, 'We are almost there, we are almost there.' I was getting hungry and it was two hours late and I was about to go
home and then they finally arrived. I walk outside and Brad
comes out and opens the door, and I am like. 'That's not him,
it's gotta be someone that looks like him.' But I am being all
cool because I am used to reading famous people. So I get
inside the limo and he introduces me to her and he calls her
'Angie,' and I am like that cannot be her, either—she looks too
skinny. I am tripping in my head. He tells me it is her birthday.
By now, I have gotten a good look at her and I know for sure
it is Angelina. She was surprised, had no idea this was gonna
be happening, and she asked him how he found me and Brad
said he asked a friend, who said I am the best psychic in L.A.
Brad goes to Angelina, 'I wouldn't bring you to just anyone!' "

"Were you nervous?"

"Well, I had never met them, but on TV—it was actually *E!
News*—I had predicted Brad and Angelina would get married.
This was just after he left Jen Aniston. I was asked by the in-
terviewer who Brad will be with after Jen, and I said it would
be a dark-haired woman who is around him. Six months later,
I am getting groceries and I see one of those magazines and
there's a picture of Brad and Angelina together!"

"Did they know you predicted this?" I ask.

"I don't think so, but I didn't ask." Deseret shrugs.

"So you're in the limo . . ."

"Yeah," she says. "Just the three of us in the back. It was
one of those long limos. It was weird. Because Brad said, 'Can

you read her first?' So I take a piece of paper and I tell her to sign it. So she does. So she signs her name. I can read people's signatures. It tells me a lot. But I also had my cards. So I read her and she is looking at me the entire time. She is very sweet and has an amazing soul. You could see the light come out of her and she said, 'How do you know all these things?' I tell her that I have been doing this for a while da-da-da and I give her my story of how I started. And you know what? Everything I said to her happened."

"What did you tell her?"

"I don't want to share everything with you; that wouldn't be right."

"I understand. But was this before she was diagnosed with breast cancer?"

"Yes, it was. I told her she was having surgery, but I didn't touch much on that. She didn't ask about her health. She just said, 'What do you see?' And I saw her having a surgery and told her that. I then read Brad and that was it. We drove around L.A. for about an hour. The driver took us back to my shop to drop me off. They gave me a hug, tipped me really well, and drove off."

At this point, I've been sitting across from Deseret for a half an hour listening rapt to her storytelling. She is captivating and it's easy to see why she often makes TV and radio appearances. But while hearing about Brangelina is interesting, I am here to find out what she sees in me. I want to find God, get answers, come to peace, I tell her. "So can you read me?" I ask.

"Of course," she says, immediately sliding open a desk drawer so quickly as if she's saying, *I thought you'd never ask.*

In a very precise, ritualistic manner, Deseret pulls out a

deck of cards and places them in front of her, then she takes a crystal from another drawer and bangs it on the desk.

"Don't touch this one," she instructs me, placing it between us, explaining the crystal was given to her by a healer in Brazil who "charged" it especially for her.

Deseret places several shiny, black stones next to the crystal. "Sometimes I get information out of them and sometimes I don't," she explains. "But I pull them out when I channel."

She puts on a pair of glasses and begins shuffling the deck of cards like a poker dealer. Each card has a design on it, but they are so worn and faded I can barely make out the images.

"These are tarot cards. They are very old. My deck tap dances and speaks and when I lay them on the table, a portal opens up. I get the information from the vibration of the cards."

She stops shuffling and puts them into two piles. "I want you to pick a pile," she says. "The stack that you pick is the stack I will flip over and read. The one that I flip over tells me a different story of your life. This is how I get a very accurate reading."

I pick the one on the left and she shuffles that pile, banging them hard on the desk several times before each fan and laying them out in three piles between us.

She puts a piece of stationery and a pen on the desk in front of her. "Now I am going to need your full name as it appears on your birth certificate, and your birthday," she says.

I tell her "Kenneth Joel Baker" and April 18, 1970, which she writes down on the paper.

"Pick one of those three piles," she says.

I pick the middle one, which she inserts amid the other two stacks and begins aggressively shuffling, staring into my eyes as if in a trance. She shuffles and reshuffles the cards for about a minute. I just watch.

She then bangs the deck very hard on the desk three times and puts them down, fanning them open. As she is staring at the cards, she suddenly blurts in a tone lower than her normal voice, "It says that at this point in your path, in your life, you are becoming a lot stronger. You're awakening three aspects of your life that you are not familiar with and you are confused. It's almost like you are discovering gifts that you have hidden that you haven't really tapped into.

"The cards are showing that on an emotional level you find yourself where you are not necessarily grounded or stable and you have to deal with your own fears and stabilize yourself in a spiritual aspect.

"This is saying you have a need on a spiritual aspect and you are trying to fulfill that need the best way you know how, which would be to react by doing something on a physical aspect. And the way you know how is to write a book and you will have a new project. And that is sort of like the logical part of yourself but in the spiritual realm what that says is that you have to start paying attention to this gift; it is time to start tapping into it, pay attention to your spiritual needs and the gifts that you have, work that muscle, make it strong so that you can understand it and open up a new door. What we usually call it is that you are going through a period of awakening."

She keeps staring at the cards. "Hmm." She looks up at me over the top of her glasses. "This is very interesting."

"What?" I ask eagerly.

"This is actually very cool," she says, glancing back at the cards. "It says that both aspects, the physical and the nonphysical, are not in harmony, are not in balance, so you are finally trying to balance it."

I tell her I hadn't done yoga in a few years, but recently

began taking a class once a week. "Keep doing that," she says. "This will be an important part of your journey."

As she glances back at the cards she keeps talking. "It says that you are very analytical. And you are very 'two plus two is four' because that is what science says. It's like, if it is not in front of you and doesn't make sense in the way that you have been taught how, then you don't understand it. But you are going to start seeing things in a three-dimensional level and understand what is behind all that. Does that make any sense?"

I nod yes. But I don't say anything. I don't want to tip her off and lead her. Skeptics say psychics are just gifted at being intuitive, that someone like Deseret is actually "reading" people—not cards.

She continues, "And this spirit quest you are on, I am seeing that the main thing is that it is a door, a gateway for you to start changing. It says that through that change there is a lot of healing that you will be doing."

She adds, "Your cards look pretty good though. Usually it comes in with chaos energy and I don't see that."

Deseret gathers the cards and reshuffles them several times. As she handles the cards, mixing them up into random order, I ask her why some mediums use cards and some don't. "You carry an energy and send it out to me," she explains. "I disconnect from your energy field, and, rather connect with you directly, I come around to you the back way. I am not getting it from this, but from a portal that reads you, but not directly."

"Are there things you can read from me directly?" I ask.

"Yes." She places a blank piece of paper in front of me on the desk. "Sign that."

"My name?"

"No, my name!" She giggles. "Of course, your name."

So I do and slide the signed paper back to her.

She stares at it. Then looks me in the eye.

"You overanalyze everything," she says. "It's like it doesn't even let you sleep. You're constantly thinking about it. You judge yourself better than anyone else, to the point that it blocks you sometimes. It's like too much. You can't even sleep."

"That's interesting you say that," I tell her.

"Why?" she asks.

"It is true. I have been having trouble sleeping."

"Getting in touch with your inner spirit, what you are doing, will calm you. It should help."

"It hasn't yet really."

"It will."

She looks at the cards. "You are very detached though. It is hard to get you to emotionally commit yourself because you're very methodical. It's like everything has to add up and make sense in your head. You don't want to let emotions drive it. You are driven by facts. Everything is organized in your head. Things have to meet certain criteria in order for you to proceed. You're going to learn to follow your intuition more."

"I have been meditating, trying to do at least ten minutes a day," I tell her.

"Good," she says. "That will open up your third eye."

Deseret shuffles the cards again. She splays them out. "I see that you have slowed yourself down since you turned thirty-three. That's when you really started to organize and put things in compartments."

"That's pretty interesting," I reply. "That's how old I was when my first child was born."

Until that last comment about my changing at age thirty-three, I felt like a lot of what Deseret had said could be intuited from what I had told her or she could have looked up. Although I never shared the age of my oldest child, or how old I was when he was born, I suppose it could have been a hunch or a guess on her part, not necessarily a paranormal vision. Is she legit? I'm not sure. Some things are spot-on, yet a lot of her observations are rather generic and apply to anyone who is on a journey to become more spiritually minded, which I had told her about.

"Anything else you want to know?" she asks.

It's been close to an hour since we began. I don't want to take up any more of her time. But there is something, while I have her here. She is a fortune-teller, after all.

"Will I find the spiritual answers I am looking for?" I ask her.

"What the spirit is telling me is that you are on the right path," she says. "But you have to turn off your mind. It is getting in the way. Doing this will open you up. Until then, it will be like you are banging your head against the wall. But when you finally trust your inner voice, your true self, your life will change entirely."

I thank her for her time. She stands and shakes my hand. "It's my pleasure," she replies. "It's what I do."

"I know you said you wouldn't charge me, but I want to pay you," I say.

"No, no," she says. "That's not necessary."

"But at least I want to pay you for your time."

"Really, it's OK. I just want you to find your spirit guide."

Exodus

I had opened my heart and mind in a quest to truly know my spiritual self. I began feeling more connected to my soul.

And then, one day, at Pastor Judah's Bible study in Beverly Hills, I learned that "gossip"—a job requirement as an E! News reporter and analyst—can be an act that takes one further from God. As my pastor noted is proclaimed in Ephesians 29: "Do not let any unwholesome talk come out of your mouths, but only what is helpful for building others up according to their needs, that it may benefit those who listen."

This insight sparked a crisis of conscience, and I wondered, What if my spiritual journey leads me to conclude I can no longer gossip about public people's private lives? How then will I provide for my family? What gifts could I share with the world that would bring love and kindness ... and money?

While I longed for spiritual freedom, I feared my life's work was now amounting to a slavery of my soul, from which I might have to perform an exodus from Hollywood, unless I could reconcile my inner conflict.

Indeed, despite making progress, I still had many questions. And sensing the answers would be found by probing deeper on the inside, I remained committed to turning my gaze within— praying, seeking, asking, listening, and meditating until I found answers to the soul-seeking questions that might part the turbulent seas separating me from a more promised land.

XI

TAKE A WALK ON "THE OTHER SIDE" OF HOLLYWOOD

After meeting with Deseret Tavares, I decide to consult another psychic.

Although Deseret offered broad predictions and insights into my life, as of now I don't have any context to interpret the reading as true or false. But if I see another psychic, perhaps they will provide a control, sort of like in a scientific experiment. I reason that by seeing a second person, I will have some comparable "data" to analyze before drawing any conclusions about all this paranormal activity and fortune-telling mumbo-jumbo.

Fortunately, I have lucked upon access to a highly sought-after celebrity psychic named Tyler Henry, a twenty-year-old clairvoyant specializing in talking to those who have "passed on." His popularity has recently skyrocketed due to the launch of a hit show on E! titled, *Hollywood Medium*.

Since Tyler and I share the same network publicist, I reach out to him and ask if Tyler will be coming into the E! offices anytime soon, and, if so, could I have a sit-down with him. Tyler has said yes.

So after having gone forty-six years of my life and only seeing one psychic (that breakup-predicting lady in Manhattan back in 1993), in the span of one week I will have seen two psychics.

When I greet Tyler in the E! lobby my first impression is a common shallow one: The slim, pale young man in the button-down shirt and black old-man slacks is shorter than he looks on TV. Of course, everyone always says this about male celebrities. Embarrassingly enough, after twenty years of meeting celebs, I still say that too.

"Hello," Tyler says formally. As we shake hands his grip is so weak, his hand so brittle, that I fear I may break it.

I notice he is wearing makeup, having apparently just come from a shoot, and his blond hair is parted sharply to the side.

I walk him upstairs to my office, small-talking about the Kardashians and how he is going to overtake them in the ratings. He guffaws. Once inside my office, I offer him a seat on my couch. I notice Tyler's forehead is glistening. I apologize for it being so warm in my office today. He smiles and shimmies out of his black sport coat. "I'm going to take this off," Tyler says. "I always get hot."

"I've noticed on your show that you sweat a lot during readings," I tell him.

"It is a very physical process." He sits gently down and delicately crosses his legs as I sit in a chair directly across from him and fold my hands.

Tyler explains, "As I start taking on symptoms and picking up on things, they can come through basically the other five senses. So I always tell people the sixth sense goes through the other five. So, in other words, I might hear a voice, I might get a smell. Or in some cases I might get a physical sensation that corresponds with how someone has passed.

"Oh," I say. "I have pictures for you! Your manager asked that I bring some to help you channel."

"Oh, awesome!" he says with such childlike chipperness he reminds me of an actor on *Glee*.

I hand him a photo album. "This was a picture book my wife put together for my fortieth birthday."

"Wonderful," he says, placing it on his lap without even looking at it.

He reaches into his leather bag and pulls out a sketchpad and a pen. "What I will do is scribble and let you know what kind of stuff pops in and we will go from there and go all over the place. If anything makes sense, let me know. If something doesn't, let me know too. We will go all over."

"Sounds good," I say. Sticking to the same skeptic's plan as I did with Deseret and being reticent about revealing too much to him, I add, "I'm ready."

Tyler stares down at the floor to my right foot and begins furiously scribbling, mumbling an occasional "OK" and "hmm" and "interesting" as I watch him silently.

"OK," he says suddenly. "I feel I am inclined to talk about your mom's side of the family initially, as this is who is coming through. Is that OK?"

"Yeah, whatever you want."

"I feel that on your mom's side of the family there is a reference to a father figure." Tyler still is not making eye contact as he scratches seemingly random shapes onto the paper. "So, OK yeah. I am going to Mom's side and we have a man coming through for your mother. Which would mean your mother would still have to be alive. So your mother is still living. Is that right?"

"Yes," I reply. She is." Maybe just a good guess—or he's read my Facebook page.

"She has a man that is insistent to come through for her right now," Tyler adds. "He's making reference to 'the five kids.' And then 'the three kids.' But it's all on that side of the family. So . . . does this mean anything to you?"

"My God, that is crazy," I say, my stone face melting as I realize that right out of the gate he has tapped into a Ken Baker Family fun fact that is not Google-able. "My mom has five kids. And she has three stepkids."

"This man who is coming through is one of the primary energies I am connected to. The impression he is giving me when it comes to his passing is that he acknowledges that when some of his grandkids were born, like, he was really old by the time his grandkids were born. He is making an emphasis to say he didn't feel like he was a young grandfather. For whatever reason, he is acknowledging a feeling of being older."

"I'm not sure what you are saying."

Tyler pinches his brow and looks up. "How do I word this? It's almost like he's acknowledging . . ."

"Wait," I interrupt. "Who is this man talking to you?

"This would be your grandfather on your mom's side."

"OK," I say, masking my shock that he would know that my mother's father died at age seventy-five when I was just five and that my memories of him are of a cancer-ridden old man in a wheelchair who couldn't play with me. Tyler's depiction is spot-on.

As I bite my tongue, Tyler continues, "The way this comes through is that he has a closer relationship with his children on

the other side than he did in real life. Because he is acknowledging that he didn't get the chance in his life to really get to
know them."

"Well, that is really true," I reveal. "My mother was raised
by a single mom who didn't really know him that well most
of his life."

"Then that makes sense," Tyler says with a friendly grin,
then closes his eyes, pauses, and adds, "There is a reference to
this that I want to talk about, and it is that he establishes a way
closer to connection to family on the other side than in this
life. The man, your grandfather, that is giving me reference to
wait—" Tyler cocks his head like a confused poodle. "Sorry,
two people are talking at once. OK. He is coming through
and referencing either an Erb or maybe a Herb."

I feel the blood rush from my face. I stare at Tyler. Speech-
less.

"OK, he is referencing, I am getting, the name Herb," Tyler
continues.

"Herb was my grandfather's name, Tyler," I share. "Herbert
Murphy."

"Oh, great," Tyler says matter-of-factly. "So this is who we
are connecting with right now."

As Tyler returns to scribbling on his pad, I mentally rifle
through how he would know my grandfather's name was
Herb and how he would know my mom wasn't close with
him. I realize I had mentioned this family fact in a memoir
I wrote back in 2001. Could he have read my book before
meeting with me? Possible.

"Do you know if there are any alcoholics on your mom's
side of the family?" Tyler asks.

"Yes," I reply. "Her brother."

I've never revealed that about Uncle Ron.

"OK, the way this is coming across is that I have a reference from him to geographical difference between you and this side of the family. There is a reference to her brother and where is he currently?"

"He lives an hour away from my mom."

"So where would your mom be living currently?"

"In Buffalo, New York."

"So you are separated from them currently."

"Yes."

"OK, sooo," Tyler's face is now beading with sweat, his pale cheeks tinged pink. "There is a reference to alcoholism—there is one living alcoholic who is a man."

"That would make sense about my uncle Ron," I say.

Tyler adds, "That is your uncle on your mother's side. Just good to keep that in mind."

Tyler scribbles away for a minute before stopping and sighing. "I have a person coming through who passed away from cancer. They are making an insistent focus on referencing the two kids, the two kids."

"Well, I have two kids."

"OK, so you have two kids currently." He scribbles more and mumbles several OKs before stopping as if he is frustrated that he is having trouble communicating with this apparent dead person.

"I apologize, but readings can be like a puzzle and we have to figure it out," he says. "Someone is coming through who is a fatherly figure but he is acknowledging himself as not being on your mom's side. I am sensing paternal, paternal. This is a new individual coming through. This man is making his presence known that he is here now.

"He is making a reference to hockey," Tyler says.

"Well, I have always played hockey. My kids play hockey. It is a big part of my life. My dad was really into my hockey."

"OK, so on your dad's side, do you know who his two brothers would be?"

"My dad had two brothers."

"They are both dead," Tyler states as fact, though I am not sure how he would know such a thing, seeing as though my uncles (one was the town dog catcher) were about as far from being public figures as you could get. "And I'm getting that one of his brothers had the same biological mother and father."

"Yes, his brother Lynn just died this year."

"Did anyone deal with a heart-related issue or challenge?"

"They all did," I say, swallowing a lump in my throat that is emotionally welling up. "All of them. And diabetes."

"I am so sorry," Tyler says with a sensitive pursing of his lips.

"It's OK, I was super close to my dad, but not really my uncles," I say.

"I quickly want to talk about health for you," Tyler tells me. "I want to mention that you have to keep in mind that you have susceptibility to an inflammatory thing. I am going to describe this as best I can. There is a reference to an inflammation-based disorder. Or an inflammatory-related thing that would generally involve joints but it is more than that."

"Well, I have arthritis in my right hip," I say. "It's often really painful."

Tyler says, "You are a little young to be getting arthritis."

"Yeah, but it is from hockey, from repetitive strain. I have to be on top of it and keep it loose and strengthened. If I don't, I am limping."

"Keep in mind to get yours checked—and there is also

reference to one eye being worse than the other and progressive decline so one being worse, and one declining in one eye."

OK, now Tyler is pulling out deep background medical stuff about me that I have never shared publicly. I want to stand up in my office and shout, "You've passed the test!" But instead I just keep passively answering his questions, to judge his overall performance before grading him.

"My right eye is really weaker than my left," I explain. "It's tricky to get glasses that work for both eyes. That would be correct what you are saying."

"I am not worried about it, but keep an eye on it, so to speak," Tyler says. "But I am getting something, a susceptibility you might have to possibly testicular cancer or tumors or something along those lines."

"I don't have any testicles," I reply, adding with a laugh, "just kidding."

Tyler guns out a hearty ha-ha-ha, but turning serious adds, "I would get checked regularly. The reference is to the endocrine system and or lymphatic system."

"I do have a small benign tumor on my pituitary gland, and I have to keep it monitored. But this situation is a big deal because if I don't keep track of my hormone levels, it could affect my sexual function. So maybe that is what you are picking up on."

"None of it worries me much, but just watch it."

We've been talking for almost a half an hour now and, quite honestly, I am impressed with Tyler's insights and knowledge about my personal life and family. Either he is legit, or he had a team of researchers and private eyes investigate me beforehand, though this seems less and less likely.

Tyler flops his hands on his lap. "Any other questions," he asks.

"Yes," I say. "I want to go back to this man you talked about a few minutes ago. You said he was a fatherly figure. I'm wondering if my father is trying to come through. He died twenty-two years ago. He was my best friend."

"Sure, sure," Tyler says eagerly. "What was his first name?"

"Larry." My stomach is tense. If Tyler is able to channel my late father in a believable way, I am not sure how I will react emotionally. I could easily become a sobbing mess just like the celebrities do when he reads them on his E! reality show.

"OK," Tyler says while sketching. "Let's see if we can get anything on that at all. . . ."

Tyler looks away to his left and draws circles and lines and shapes on his sketchpad as if in an artistic trance.

"OK," Tyler says about thirty seconds into his trance. "The man is snapping his fingers. Like, snap, snap, snap. Whoever this is, he is snapping, referencing that his transition went way too quick or fast. He is snapping. It was a quick transition from here to the other side."

"I don't know if this is it, but my dad always snapped his fingers, and taught me how to snap, and he was pretty young when he passed. Actually, he was fifty-one when he died."

"Yes, there is a reference . . . hold on . . . who had the stroke on that side of the family?" Tyler looks at me quizzically. "He is having me say 'stroke.'"

"Who is 'he'?" I ask.

"This would be your father."

My face grows hot. "My father's dad died from a stroke," I say.

"Well, I have with me here a man who died from a stroke and a man who died from lung cancer."

"My dad died from lung cancer," I reveal, my eyes welling with tears.

"The stroke and the lung cancer are coming through," Tyler says. "They are together."

I am in shock and blink back tears.

"Hmm." Tyler cocks his head. "Your dad keeps saying, 'Philadelphia.'"

The word doesn't ring any bells for me, other than that I have visited the City of Brotherly Love a couple of times.

"And, OK," Tyler continues with a grave expression, his cheeks growing redder. "I keep getting a reference to the lung cancer thing. The reference to this is that he is saying, 'I either got misdiagnosed initially or there was an issue about the timing.' There is an acknowledgment of either, 'I go for a test and I got told I had something else and I go back and actually get diagnosed with lung cancer.'"

I tell him, "My dad had been coughing a lot because he had smoked all his life, and I remember he had gotten a lung scan and was boasting about how the doctor told him his lungs were 'clear.' Then a few months later, he went back in and they found he had lung cancer and it had already spread. He died a year later."

"Right, yes, OK," Tyler says, closing his eyes. He opens them. "Yeah, he is referencing this, but he is acknowledging a sense of closure or peace with the people that he is referencing, and they are your siblings. He keeps talking about 'the five' and he is saying, 'I have closure.' There is an acknowledgment though that he knows he was given permission to pass away. And that he could go."

I am trembling and wipe tears from my cheek with my forearm, smearing my beige TV-ready makeup on my sleeve.

"When he died, all my brothers were there with him, he was unconscious, and they told him he could go, that it was OK for him to die. I wasn't there."

Then it hits me like a brick to my heart.

"Tyler, why did you say, 'Philadelphia'?" I ask.

"Well, I didn't say that—your dad did," Tyler says with a gentle smile.

"Holy smokes!" I smack my hands to my thighs. "I just realized that when my father lost consciousness, I hopped on a plane to get home to Buffalo. I had to make a connection and when I landed at the airport, I rushed to a pay phone and called my mom. She told me, 'Kenny, I am sorry but your father just died at the hospital.'" I bite my lower lip. I press the tears back. "And I had totally forgotten until now that the airport I was in when I found out he died was in Philadelphia.

"Oh, my gosh, Tyler." I am now a blubbering mess. "My brothers told him to go, Tyler. I couldn't make it home in time. I felt terrible."

"Just know that he is with you and that he is proud of you. And he loves you so much."

"That is amazing, Tyler. No one knows that Philadelphia thing, that level of detail. I had totally forgotten myself where I was when he died. My gosh. You have a gift that is incredible."

"Thank you," Tyler says. "I can't emphasize enough what is so beautiful is the connection and knowing that he is around you always. And when he comes through he is making a point right now of telling you how proud of you he is and he has gotten to see you and your kids. That's big for him. That's really big for him. He is definitely aware of that. And as he comes through he is sharing that love and acknowledgment. He sees it all. Everything."

"Tyler, this is very powerful to me." I get up and grab a tissue off my desk and blow my nose.

"Just know that his connection to you is so strong that he didn't need to have you actually be physically present there to say goodbye. He says he feels like he had a lifetime of time he got to spend with you. To him, that was closure. So please know that he is around."

After clearing out my nose and wiping dry my tears, I see Tyler out to the E! lobby and wrap a big hug around his bony body. "I can't thank you enough," I tell him. "You really blew me away. You've given me a lot to think about."

I scurry back up to my office, feeling a sense of calm and relief. Until now, I had thought I had grieved and processed my dad's death, but after seemingly getting communication from him I realize I hadn't fully healed. I needed to hear from him. The word to describe what I feel is . . . grace.

But that couldn't be real. Tyler must be an illusionist. How could someone possibly communicate with a dead person? It seems the stuff of magic and fantasy.

My creeping doubts getting the best of me, I call my mother back in Buffalo and tell her what I have just experienced. Then, believing that maybe my brain convinced itself it was Philadelphia, I ask my mom the single fact Tyler knew that blew me away most.

"Mom, do you remember when I called you from an airport and you told me that Dad died?"

"Yes," she replies. "Of course, I do."

"Do you remember what city I was in?" I ask.

Without pause, Mom replies, "Philadelphia."

XII

KNOW GOD AND YOU SHALL FIND GOD

(BEHOLD THE BIBLE IN BEVERLY HILLS)

Turns out that I am not the only one in the *E! News* room impressed by Tyler Henry's apparent spiritual gifts. When word leaks out that I had just received a reading from the celebrity psychic, coworkers start peppering me with questions: *Is he for real?* [Yes!] *What did he tell you?* [He talked to my dead dad!] *Can you get me a reading with him?* [Probably not.]

Over the years we've had the biggest stars in the world parade through our offices and, with the exception of when Michelle Obama, flanked by an army of Secret Service agents, came for an interview, I have never seen my work friends so star struck.

As for me, I'm still in shock at the accuracy and insight of Tyler's reading. I have gone my whole life believing that psychics were a fraud, that they just used intuition and guesswork, preying on people who desperately want to believe they can talk to the dead. But I am not that person. Although I was open-minded, and a week ago Deseret Tavares had intrigued me with some of her comments, I expected Tyler to be more of a magician than a psychic mentalist.

I must make sense of Tyler's gift, not to mention process that my father's spirit really might be around me.

I text Pastor Judah Smith. He has a Bible study session tonight at the Four Seasons in Beverly Hills. I wasn't planning to go tonight, but now I feel a pull to seek answers. And since Judah has been a mentor for me on this journey, I text:

> Judah—might you have a few minutes before the service tonight to meet with me? It's fairly urgent. Could use your help.

He replies immediately:

> *Of course, my friend. Let's meet up backstage before bible study . . .*

It's three o'clock, but Judah's Bible study doesn't start until seven. My psychic encounter is consuming me as I breeze through writing my news stories for the day and we tape our show: Kylie Jenner's boyfriend might have his Lamborghini repossessed . . . Kesha is still fighting with her record label . . . Lea Michele got two new tattoos . . . Khloe Kardashian Instagrammed a photo of her tiny waist while her sister Kim joined the "Mile-High Club" . . .

All this "news" seems so silly in the wake of the intense spiritual experience with Tyler. In fact, it seems inconsequential nearly all the time. But now even more than ever. There is a deeper, more soulful place to tap into life. Rather than distracting people from the most meaningful experiences of life, I feel as if I should be doing the opposite. But I am not. I sling gossip about famous people, I talk about last night's Real

Housewives catfight, I dissect whether Kanye West can make a comeback and if his Yeezy sneakers are cool or not.

I must be meant for something more. This can't be my life's purpose, could it? And if it is, then God has a sick sense of humor. But where would I even start to embark on a more spiritually enlightened professional life? First off, I don't even know what I really believe. Do I now believe in ghosts? Do I believe Jesus was the son of God and died for our sins? Or am I at heart a Buddhist who finds God in a breath? Maybe I am just a lost agnostic, sitting on the faith fence over what I want, need, and desire.

At last, I wrap *E! News* and drive three miles east down Wilshire Boulevard and park on the residential street behind the Four Seasons. I walk into the lobby of the opulent main ballroom and wait for Pastor Judah to arrive. As I sit watching the well-groomed Christians file in, looking so happy and content and proud of themselves for taking time out of their L.A. lives to nurture their soul, I feel a little better about things. I have a sense that while I am far from "finding God," I think I am on the right path, that I am gradually changing. Maybe the other psychic, Deseret, was right when she said, "This spirit quest you are on, I am seeing that the main thing is that it is a door, a gateway for you to start changing. It says that through that change there is a lot of healing that you will be doing."

I am reaching out for help, opening my heart, and seeking truth. Maybe that's what my spiritual quest is all about. "Finding" God may be all about the journey, with the destination only ever being found after death. But I really don't know either way.

I remain confused by Tyler's apparent paranormal powers

and how they fit in with my beliefs. But I trust Judah to give me his honest take. I want to ask him how to understand what just happened not only from a Christian-based perspective, but from a secular, intellectual place as well.

A few minutes later, Judah texts me.

Hey man. I am here. Come around the back.

I enter the ballroom and walk to stage left, push through a curtain break, and find Judah sitting in a makeshift green room.

He hugs me.

"Thanks for seeing me," I say, sounding like a patient seeing a doctor for an emergency visit, which this is.

"Let's sit down," Judah says.

We sit on folding chairs, Judah scootches his close to me. He leans forward with his forearms resting on his thighs.

"OK, man," I begin. "I know this is going to sound weird, but have you heard of the psychic Tyler Henry, the guy on the E! channel?"

"Yeah, I've heard of him, but never watched him."

"OK, so I wasn't planning on having the supernatural or mysticism be part of my journey, but a friend was like, You have to talk to a psychic. I figured, well, so many people in Hollywood believe in this stuff, maybe I should experience it. I didn't believe in psychics or astrology—it's all goofy to me." My mouth is moving a million miles an hour. "But today, this Tyler Henry kid came to my office and said stuff that blew me away. But not a just a mentalist, intuitive kind of thing. This seemed very real, Judah. Like, OK, my dad died, and Tyler was talking about the day he died and he randomly said, 'I see Philadelphia,' and Tyler goes, 'It's OK, don't worry that you weren't there when he died.' I had to think hard and then it hit me that I had totally forgotten this, but when he died I had flown on a plane to Philadelphia and landed at that airport and my mom told me he died. So I am like, How the eff does he know this? I mean, I have never told anyone, never wrote about this, and I didn't even remember that happening until he said it. So I wanted to get your opinion. How do you explain this kind of thing? Because it seems so legit and real that it is really messing with me."

Judah has sat silently nodding as my mouth motored through the story. He sighs and says, "Ken, the Bible says the gifts of God come without repentance. Tyler has a gift from God. It's from God. Whether he believes in God or not, God doesn't take our gifts away because we don't believe in Him. Kobe Bryant, we celebrate his gift. Kobe can believe in God or not, but God gave him a gift to play ball."

"I can believe that, but I was raised Catholic, and taught to stay away from this stuff. I was always told it was the work of Satan blah-blah-bah . . ."

"But the Bible teaches that greater is he that is within us," Judah says. "Ghosts and goblins and devils and demons—I don't fear them at all. I am full of Jesus. For me, Tyler is not an intimidating figure. I believe Jesus is my savior. I believe Tyler has a prophetic gift as a prophet; Tyler has a gift from God. So he has a gift where he can see, where he can feel people and get ideas from people's past and future, I get that. But in my opinion if Tyler experienced the forgiveness of Jesus and love of Jesus I think he would really discover what his gift is ultimately all about."

"So you think a psychic medium can be a real phenomenon?" I ask.

"Yes, I have seen this, and I believe it can be real," Judah says. "I think it is interesting and exhilarating to see people with gifts—even apart from God—because those gifts are still there from God. That shows incredible mercy on God's part. Because if I was God and you were showing off these spiritual gifts but not to glorify me but maybe to entertain and inform only, then I am going to take these away. But you know what, God never does that. He has endless mercy and love and so He gives us these gifts and remains faithful and kind and gracious."

"I really wish you were my pastor growing up," I tell him. "When I was little in Catholic church, I feel like I was made to fear God, made to think He was vengeful and if I didn't follow His commandments that I would go to hell. The message of love was totally lost on me."

Judah laughs. "Sorry you had that experience, but unfortunately it is a common one. The scriptures were written by forty-plus people over sixteen hundred years. You go to the Koran, the Book of Mormon, and you have one person writing it from one vantage point from one generation. But in the Bible, we have a book here that is so supernatural, it is the undisputed bestselling book of all time, and has a message that is unparalleled by any. Sadly, it has been used to abuse and enslave and kill and destroy and marginalize. The Bible has been used to hurt people—by humans, not God. And there were the Christian crusaders, and we could go on and on. They did despicable things and did horrible things, but just because things were done in the name of Jesus doesn't mean that's who Jesus is."

I have caught my breath listening to Judah. I am truly hearing him. His faith is so heartfelt and real that while I may not hold such a firm, blanket belief as he does, I respect, admire and trust him. It makes me appreciate, perhaps even *know* the Christian message in a way that I have never before.

"Judah, I gotta be honest," I say. "I am more open than I have ever been in my life. I have felt a lot of pain and fear and anxiety in my life, but being here, with you, listening to you, I feel like your professing and explaining your faith is an act of healing for me."

"That's beautiful, man," he says. "Praise Jesus."

"But I have to say that every time I feel as though I am having a quote-unquote born-again experience in my heart, my brain stops me. The whole concept that Jesus is the only way to God just doesn't seem intellectually acceptable. There are so many beautiful faith traditions and many of them have merit. I was talking to this actress Taryn Manning recently, and she was telling me she was raised in the Bahá'í Faith. So I read up on it and learned that they believe in the unity of all religions, that all the major faith traditions have the same enlightened force, that their teachings all come from the same God. And you know what? I just think I can believe that more than this 'I am the only way' message from Jesus. No offense."

"Well," Judah says with a laugh. "No offense taken, because what you just said is so beautiful and important. Let's break this down a little." Judah sits up straight. "First of all, we have the claim of Jesus and, you are right, it is an exclusive one. It's like when you break an exclusive story on *E! News*, right? Ken Baker is the only one with this report!"

"Yeah, but the news I share is far from life and death," I say.

"Perhaps," Judah says. "But my point is that God says, 'I am the way, the truth, the light. If you've seen me, I am the father. We are one.' So Jesus claims to be the promised Messiah."

"But," I interrupt, "I would be more able to follow Jesus's teachings if his teachings allowed me to accept and practice other thought leaders' lessons. I mean, maybe it is wishy-washy of me, but I feel like if I want to practice Buddhist meditation, or incorporate Hindu philosophy into my life, or even Islamic principles, why not? Because Jesus says so?"

"Well, yeah," Judah says with a shrug. "He is claiming to be the superhero, the savior of humanity."

"Well, I appreciate that, and I am not saying I *don't* believe him," I say. "But I sort of feel like Carl Sagan, in that I am not ready to declare Jesus is or isn't the messiah, because I just haven't seen enough evidence to confirm that hypothesis. I guess what I am saying is that I am not ready to take that leap of faith."

Judah nods, doesn't speak. He curls his lips in a toothless smile. A few moments later: "Look, we know there's wrong, we know there's wickedness, we know there is sin, and Jesus says I have not sinned, I do not sin, therefore I can take care of your sins. So the first thing that needs to be established is that the premise of Jesus is not what a lot of people think it is. Jesus didn't come to be one of the guys. He came to be *the* guy. He claims unanimously to be God with skin and bone on him. So Jesus doesn't play nice with other gods. And that's a little bit of a misnomer. That Jesus can kind of be one of many gods. He never claims that. That is rare among the gods, frankly. And that alone produces incredible intellectual intrigue. So Jesus teaches exclusivity. But Jesus also teaches in Hebrews 11 that faith is the substance of things hoped for, it is the evidence of things not seen. Because the universe itself—the Bible declares it—declares the glory of God and the validity and reality of Jesus. The Bible says that the cry for Utopia is within all of us. Because we were not designed for sin. Ken, we weren't designed for sin, for death, for end, for losing loved ones. This isn't what we were made for. That's why funerals are so devastating to our brains. We can't fathom it because we are inherently wired from the beginning of time to live without sin, in total unison with God. That's why every generation has this fascination with God. There is this so-called God space in all of us. But the reason I am attracted to Jesus and believe in Jesus with all my heart is Jesus is more than a mantra, Jesus is more than a dogma, Jesus is more than an idea; he's a person to be encountered and to be experienced. So this is fundamentally different than a lot of religions. Some claim interaction with spirit beings and ghosts and goblins and the dead and all of that—like you've shared about Tyler. And by the way I do believe that a lot of that is very real. The Bible even talks about Satan cloaking himself as an angel of light."

"I get that," I say. "I guess the bottom line is that why can't I believe that Tyler Henry is a legit medium, and that the Buddha and Mohammad and Jesus and other historical figures are legit prophets? Can't they all be true? I mean, just because I say, 'Hey, I am the best journalist in Hollywood,' that doesn't make me the best. You get what I am saying?"

"Yes, I do," Judah says. "And it is profound what you are asking. It is exactly what God wants you to ask. He gave you a brain to ask questions, to be skeptical, not to just blindly believe what anyone tells you. But let's use a sports analogy again, because I love sports. If Tiger Woods walked in here and you were like, 'I think I can beat you in golf,' Tiger wouldn't go, 'No you wouldn't, no you can't! I am really good. In fact, here are all the tournaments I have won, all the money I've made!' He wouldn't do that. He would chuckle and smile because he knows he is the top guy. My point being, I think people are really busy trying to defend Jesus all the time. Just turn on the TV and see these preachers selling him like a used car. But if Jesus is God, and he is not intimidated by our exploration, why should we fear other faiths, other perspectives and practices? We shouldn't.

"If you look at Jesus in all the stories, he seems to be at this restful, urgent, rhythmic-paced lifestyle. Of course he is. He is in control of the cosmos. He is not intimidated. He is not insecure. He is not fearful if you will or won't believe him. He wants us to question, he wants us to ask, he wants us to seek. Our souls were made for seeking."

"So it seems that what you're saying is I should go with it."

"Go with it!" he agrees. "Jesus wouldn't want it any other way."

"It's like that scripture that says you will know the truth and the truth shall set you free."

"Yes," Judah says. "The Greek word 'ginosko,' that is 'know.' That word 'know' is experiential. If you *know* the truth as Westerners, because we are so intellectually driven, we think that *ginosko* means a mental thing. But the reason I say let yourself go and 'go with it' is that we are made up of intellectualism but also emotions and soul and spirit and physical bodies and flesh and your whole being has to *ginosko* something. And either God reveals Himself in a knowing way—or we are doomed. So, Ken, questioning God is not a bad thing."

"So I am driving in the right lane on this journey," I say.

"Oh, my God, you are in the center of the highway! You're drafting right now in the Tour de France. You are right behind Lance Armstrong, you are right where you need to be.

"I know that we preachers like to call people to accept Jesus with a simple prayer at the end of every service, but with one prayer not everything is going to make sense. That is not how we work. There is beauty in the ambiguity, there is beauty in the questions. God works with light and clarity. So the confusion you feel is you moving away from the confusion we produce in our own life. I believe that the closer you get to Jesus, things are gonna get clearer and clearer. But enjoy the journey. Your faith is building and growing. Explore all the many rooms of your heart and soul. It is beautiful."

For the second time in the last four hours, I am brought to tears. And as the tears trickle down my face, I ask Judah for something I have never once asked anyone: "Could you pray for me?"

"Absolutely, man," he says. "This is one of my specialties."

Judah places his hand on my shoulder and closes his eyes, as do I. "Jesus, I thank you so much for my friend Ken and I just don't think it is an accident that we are here tonight talking and I just know that you are closer than we could ever have imagined. I believe with all my heart that you have stepped into Ken's soul and his mind and his will and his emotions and have become more real to him than ever before. But we just want to say that, God, like those twelve men that followed you around for three years we want to be one of those guys. We want our minutes and days and moments to be like we are taking trips with you and wanting to experience the life you designed us for. We want to live beyond ourselves. But God, in the deepest part of our being we want to know that we know you. We pray that you will reveal yourself to us so that we might know you more. God, I pray that the biblical narrative, the verses and scriptures and stories, that they will be consuming for Ken, that he will fall into the pages and it will be like he is in the stories, and he is living it and his being and mind and soul would be swimming in this ocean of beauty and your majesty.

"God, I love you so much and I love this man and I thank you for his openness. I thank you for his love for humanity. I thank you for his care and concern for people. I pray, Lord, that you will put moments in his life in the next couple of weeks that reveal yourself to him through a myriad of beautiful ways in the way that only you can do it. God, I thank you for the days that lie ahead and the days that have been. I thank you that you are not the author of confusion. I pray that you will bring clarity and insight and wisdom. Thank you, Father. You love Ken unconditionally and eternally and we thank you in Jesus's name."

"Amen," I add.

Then I open my eyes. I am still crying. But I am not sad. I am not afraid. I am not restless and anxious and confused. I may not yet have reached my spiritual destination. I may not yet know my spiritual truth. But I do know that I am at peace with my journey and, for now, not knowing.

XIII

INVESTIGATE TOM CRUISE-OLOGY

Whenever I tell friends at E! I've been dedicating much of my free time lately trying to finding out, once and for all, what spiritual beliefs I am willing to embrace, and what God I actually might be willing to praise, many inevitably ask me if I have checked out the one religion that is most synonymous with Hollywood: The Church of Scientology.

So far, my answer has been along the lines of "Are you out of your mind?!"

The reason is simple: Strictly from an outside view, Scientology scares the hell out of me. I know it is practiced by thousands (or, if you believe the Church, several millions) of people, and that the religion has a long history of using Hollywood celebrity practitioners to promote itself as a path to unlocking one's human potential and attain "wisdom, good health and immortality." The Church even has its storied "Celebrity Centre" for high-profile stars opened by its late founder L. Ron Hubbard, a 1950s-era science-fiction writer who created the religion, which has been loyally followed by Tom Cruise, John Travolta, Will Smith, Priscilla Presley, Kirstie Alley, Beck, Jenna Elfman, Erika Christensen (who has called Cruise her spiritual mentor), and many other celebrities, including former *Fox News* anchor Greta Van Susteren, whom I sat next to at Kim Kardashian's wedding to NBA player Kris Humphries (but the topic of Scientology never came up).

Although the religion's celebrity fascination is a peculiar feature of Scientology, it is not the thing that scares me about it. The problem I have is that Scientology—which has been criticized for not being a religion but rather a self-help profit center allegedly using its "church" status to dodge taxes—has been embroiled in a PR war with numerous defectors attacking the Church for what they depict as its cultlike culture and oppressive policies.

The Church's image took a serious blow with the 2015 release of the Emmy-winning documentary, *Going Clear*, which examined the shadowy world of celebrity members and gave voice to former rank-and-filers who claimed various incidents of abuse and exploitation. The Church repeatedly tried—and failed—to have the movie blocked from release. The acclaimed documentary was based on the comprehensive book of the same title by Pulitzer Prize–winning author Lawrence Wright. The book, published in 2013, delves into the history, present, and future of Scientology with great depth. Many of its revelations are disturbing—with allegations of forgeries, falsifying history, and covering up cultish human-rights abuses—but it also provides a glimpse inside the enigmatic bureaucracy, though the book depicts it as being more of a *bureaucrazy*!

Although Wright pulls no punches in his exposé, he also

offered this even-handed review of Scientology in the context of other world religions:

> Of course, no religion can prove that it is "true." There are myths and miracles at the core of every great belief system that, if held up to the harsh light of a scholar or an investigative reporter, could easily be passed off as lies. Did Mohammed really ride into Heaven on the back of his legendary transport, the steed Buraq? Did Jesus' disciples actually encounter their crucified leader after his burial? Were these miracles or visions or lies?

Wright, however, likens many of the Church of Scientology's practices to cult movements such as the Branch Davidians and Peoples Temple, as well as the Amish culture, while also comparing its charismatic leader to religious prophets such as Mormonism's founder Joseph Smith, one of the few modern spiritual leaders whose ideas have endured. In the end, Wright concludes that Scientology, despite its name, has no true basis in science and is an amalgamation of various New Age philosophies and semiscientific theories.

The sections of *Going Clear* focused on the Church's relationship with celebrities, especially Tom Cruise, are fascinating, especially for someone like me who has covered Hollywood celebrity since the mid-1990s. While an entire book could be written just on celebrity Scientologists, Wright concludes in one chapter that the Church "orients itself toward celebrity, and by doing so, the church awards famousness a value . . . [and] the church has pursued a marketing strategy that relies heavily on endorsements by celebrities, who actively promote the religion."

The downside of harnessing the power and platform of celebrities comes when a celebrity turns on you. An outspoken celebrity critic is actress and former Scientologist Leah Remini, who published a book titled *Troublemaker: Surviving Hollywood and Scientology.* Among her many critiques, Leah revealed in her memoir that in over thirty years as a member she spent upward of $5 million on the Church—on services, training, and donations to its causes—and she said the Church requires members to pay in the range of at least $500,000 to reach the highest levels of Scientology in what allegedly amounts to an elaborate pay-to-play scheme.

How did Scientology respond to Leah's attacks? They attacked *her* with an aggressive campaign to discredit her. So viciously, in fact, it only reinforced in many people's eyes that the Church and its leader, David Miscavige, deserved its shady reputation. As a journalist, the moment I realized the Church was losing its PR war (and why is a church engaging in a PR war when it could be focused on helping people?) came when it released this statement to the world media, including to me at *E! News*:

> Leah Remini has become what she once declared she never wanted to be known as: "this bitter ex-Scientologist." As *USA Today* wrote, Ms. Remini is "as famous for being an ex-Scientologist as she is as an actress." She needs to move on with her life instead of pathetically exploiting her former religion, her former friends and other celebrities for money and attention to appear relevant again . . .
>
> Scientology is the only major religion to be founded in the 20th century and emerge as a major religion in

the 21st century. The Church has grown more in the past decade than in its first 50 years combined under the ecclesiastical leadership of Mr. Miscavige, a visionary parishioners and Church staff hold in the highest regard for carrying out the legacy of the Scientology Founder through the renaissance the religion is now experiencing. Mr. Miscavige works tirelessly for the parishioners and their benefit and to aid millions through support and participation in global humanitarian initiatives and social betterment programs. The real story of the Church of Scientology, what it does, its beliefs and practices, is available at www.scientology.org.

My professional reaction to the Church's statement: Now, this is a seriously juicy Hollywood feud! As a journalist, I didn't have an agenda one way or the other—and going into my current inquiry I still don't. If people want to bash or embrace a religion, so be it. But it becomes a story when that religion unleashes their fury back on them.

Yet, admittedly, I did have a very personal reaction to the Church's statement: It made me feel yucky.

Its heavy-handedness and meanness only confirmed why I previously had no interest in even exploring a religion that did things like issuing statements defaming its defectors and critics in such a harsh way that they make Donald Trump look like Gandhi. Seriously. The Vatican has its own share of faults and transgressions (as does most every major world religion), but would the Roman Catholic Church issue a statement about a former member, branding them a "spoiled entitled diva" filled with "bitterness and anger"? Or would the Dalai Lama put a disgruntled Tibetan monk on public blast with a press release?

But then I had to check myself. Even though I find the scandal-plagued leader of Bikram Yoga to be a foul human being, I still will enjoy taking Bikram classes because I find its series of postures performed in hundred-degree heat to be healing. As such, maybe Scientology, the practice, has merit even though the leaders appear to be just as vengeful and bitter as Leah has been. Scientology, from what I have read, promotes itself as offering a scientific approach to spiritual enlightenment. There doesn't seem to be anything wrong with that stated purpose.

The more I think about it, I realize that, in the open-minded spirit of my search for meaning amid my Hollywood madness, I am not giving Scientology a fair, journalistic review. After all, as part of my spiritual quest, I have vowed to approach every spiritual practice I am drawn to with equal impartiality. I had some negative experiences with Christianity earlier in life, but that didn't stop me from returning to it with a fresh, fair look. And if I am going to bring any bias to Scientology, I should hold that from a personal experience, not from what I read in a statement or see on TV or the web.

There's no denying that the Church of Scientology's public relations track record has not been stellar and its Hollywood-centric dogma isn't exactly biblical. But to disregard it outright would be akin to banishing Catholicism because some of its leaders allowed sexual predators to prey on children for centuries.

Sure, intellectually I have trouble taking seriously a self-help-centered religion with principles that were based on a novelist's imagination/inspiration. Yet I also felt as skeptical about Tyler Henry but walked away from my reading kind of/sort of believing in psychic powers. And, lest we forget, Jesus Christ was derided as a false prophet and was persecuted for it.

Truly, I want to give Scientology a fair shake. In reality, I have only really had one personal encounter with the Church of Scientology. It was back in the mid-2000s when I was running *Us Weekly*'s West Coast editorial office and appearing part-time on TV and radio as an expert giving commentary on all things Hollywood. One day, I was paid a visit by a Church official who had come with a briefcase containing transcripts from my appearances on CNN and other shows in which I mentioned Tom Cruise, John Travolta, and Scientology. The official wanted to tell me that I had mischaracterized the Church in a few of my quotes and sound bites and he just wanted to "educate" me. He was a nice enough guy and didn't creep me out. He just seemed genuinely to want to set the record straight that in his view the Church was a legitimate spiritual resource and not a "cult," which many have suggested.

Mind you, the idea of a church (of any kind) keeping a file on what I have said, and then sending an official over to discuss my public comments about them, is definitely in the range of creepy, but still, I wasn't particularly freaked out. I would spend big chunks of my time each week fielding phone calls from publicists complaining that the magazine had gotten something wrong. The official didn't threaten me. He didn't try to brainwash me. However, he did invite me to the Church headquarters in Hollywood to learn more about the religion. Since at that time in my life I had no interest in joining any religion, let alone Tom Cruise-ology, I politely declined.

But now, some ten years later, I want to experience firsthand what the hullabaloo is all about, probe into the religion that, in Hollywood, has become so divisive yet remains so pervasive.

So I begin my examination where most modern-day inquiries start: the Internet.

The home page of the L.A. Church of Scientology website features a video in which Los Angeles is heralded as "home to the largest Scientology community on Earth."

But my first question is what is Scientology? I mean, is it really a religion? Or is it just a self-help system? Is it possibly a cult?

The Church's official website defines itself as such:

> Developed by L. Ron Hubbard, Scientology is a religion that offers a precise path leading to a complete and certain understanding of one's true spiritual nature and one's relationship to self, family, groups, Mankind, all life forms, the material universe, the spiritual universe and the Supreme Being.
>
> Scientology addresses the spirit—not the body or mind—and believes that Man is far more than a product of his environment, or his genes.
>
> Scientology comprises a body of knowledge which extends from certain fundamental truths. Prime among these are:
>
> Man is an immortal spiritual being.
>
> His experience extends well beyond a single lifetime.
>
> His capabilities are unlimited, even if not presently realized.

Scientology further holds Man to be basically good, and that his spiritual salvation depends upon himself, his fellows and his attainment of brotherhood with the universe.

Scientology is not a dogmatic religion in which one is asked to accept anything on faith alone. On the contrary, one discovers for oneself that the principles of Scientology are true by applying its principles and observing or experiencing the results.

The ultimate goal of Scientology is true spiritual enlightenment and freedom for all.

There is no mention of members paying hundreds of thousands of dollars to make it into higher levels like a pyramid scheme, no reference to signing contracts dedicating your life to the Church, nothing about aliens coming to Earth, nothing about how Tom Cruise is the next Messiah. It also doesn't mention some of the more, uh, interesting beliefs of the religion, namely that Scientologists believe that after death our thetan (soul) leaves our body, journeys to a landing station on Venus, and then is sent back to Earth, landing in the Pacific Ocean near California.

Yet judging solely by its own definition, especially the stuff about being able to follow any other faith tradition, it actually seems to be an appealing option to explore, since I am struggling with the whole notion of exclusively devoting my faith to any single tradition or dogma. Scientology, from its own website at least, appears to be an organization that is far more inclusive than Christianity.

Further clicking through the Scientology website leads me to a page listing several introductory classes one can take if they are interested in Scientology, offering classes both online and in-classroom to help you in all areas of life, such as "Relationships with Others," "Difficulties on the Job," "Communication," and "Stress, Anxiety and Depression." This last area piques my interest, seeing as though I have suffered with all three to some degree, though daily ten-minute meditations, led by my Buddhist guru on the Headspace mobile app, has calmed my brain a bit over the last month. Even so, I crave peace and calm and healing. I'm not exactly in a position to pretend I am A-OK, that I couldn't use some help. Because I do. Badly.

I sign up for a class titled "Overcoming Ups & Downs in Life," which is described as: "If someone has been doing well and suddenly worsens, it happens for a specific reason. Here are the remarkable Scientology breakthroughs that resolve it for good. With this course, you can change your life forever."

While a little over-the-top in the promise department, the class seems like it's worth a try to see what it might deliver. After all, my emotions do tend to swing, my anxiety does come and go, leaving my stomach often aching and me riding a psychological roller coaster. Plus, the class is free. What do I have to lose? It's not like they can brainwash me in two hours. So I sign up for the five p.m. class that meets next week.

I have an actress friend who had once belonged to Scientology, but we have never really discussed her experience in great detail. I never wanted to pry. But now that I am about to enter the Sunset Boulevard compound on my own, I want to ask her about her experience with the Church. I call her up and explain that I will be taking a class.

"Be careful, Ken," she warns.

"Why?" I ask.

"Because there are some cultlike qualities to it," she says. "Not everyone there is bad, and I got a lot out of some of the classes, especially the communications courses. I did some auditing sessions that helped me clear some things in my mind."

"I've read about the auditing," I say. "They use that E-meter thing, right?"

"Yeah," she says. "They have you hold on to these metal rods, they call them cans, that are connected to a sensor that supposedly can detect your energy levels. A lot of people think it's kind of bullshit, but I found the process helpful because it's kind of like therapy in a way. What happens is the auditor asks you a series of questions, usually just general questions about whether you are upset about something, or if you are ashamed of something you've kept secret, that sort of thing. They will ask the same question over and over, and the whole idea is that you eventually release negative energy and can become 'clear.'"

"So it's like therapy," I say.

"Basically," she says. "But after all my experience there, and I did it for a few years off and on, I realized it was cultish."

"Like how?" I ask.

"There is something within that infrastructure, Ken. Not everyone is bad there at all. I know some great people, but there is something within that infrastructure that is not good. There are some bad eggs in there, and that scared me."

"You mean, the higher-ups?" I ask.

"Yeah," she says. "I spent a lot of time at the Celebrity Centre and all the other actors I met there were great. They just wanted to become better people. The whole idea that we are spiritual beings and we have incredible powers within us that we can access through the Scientology principles is appealing.

But it was not my intention to go up through the ranks, yet they push you to do that. They make you feel like you are not healed or whole unless you keep paying for more classes and buying more books. It was like, 'Oh, you are doing better, but you are only operating at ten percent of your capacity.' And the more I got into it, the more they would tell me that I had to give up any other faiths. But I am the kind of person where I don't like to rely too much on anything. I like to rely on myself. I started to feel like it was gonna be a never-ending process and I feared it could drain me financially."

"Well, that does sound like either a cult or a money-making scam—or both," I say.

"I am not saying it is all bad," she says. "But I had to tell them to stop calling me, stop emailing me, and, honestly, once I told them I was done they did leave me alone."

"Did you sign a contract?" I ask.

"Unfortunately, I did. I never thought much about it. As an actor you are always signing releases and things, and I just thought it was a waiver. I probably should have read it more closely, but it was right at the beginning and they sort of trick you into it. That was definitely something that rubbed me the wrong way. But you should go look into it for yourself. Just be careful."

My friend's admonition hasn't eased my anxiety about trying out Scientology. But it also hasn't dissuaded me from giving it a go. If anything, I am now more curious to learn firsthand about this much-gossiped-about Hollywood religion.

A week after I signed up for the class on "Overcoming Ups & Downs in Life," the day comes. All day at work, I am anxious, the knots in my stomach that had been loosening with my meditation ten minutes a day are back. I feel queasy and skip lunch.

I somehow make it through the day to tape the show, with my final segment being a hit from my desk in the E! newsroom of the day's top stories that I read straight off the Teleprompter:

[KEN ON CAMERA]
COCO'S SEX LIFE HAS TAKEN A VERY, VERY SAD TURN: IT'S NONEXISTENT!

[—VO—]
THE 37-YEAR-OLD NEW MOM TELLS "PEOPLE" SINCE THEIR FOUR-MONTH-OLD DAUGHTER, CHANEL, WAS BORN, THEY HAVE NOT FOUND TIME FOR SEX!
SHE SAYS EVERYTHING IS ABOUT THE CHILD AND NOTH-ING IS SEXUAL.

[KEN ON CAMERA]
ARIANA GRANDE HAD A BRUSH WITH DEATH!

(—VO—)
THE 22-YEAR-OLD DISHED THE SCARY DETAILS ON ALAN CARR'S CHATTY MAN, EXPLAINING LAST YEAR DURING A CONCERT SHE WAS ALMOST CRUSHED BY A MOVING STAGE!
HER GUITARIST HELPED HER OUT AND SAVED HER!

[KEN ON CAMERA]
AND LADIES, I KNOW YOU'RE DYING TO KNOW . . . DOES NICK JONAS PREFER BOXERS . . . OR BRIEFS?

(—VO—)
IN A Q & A ON "REDDIT" THE SINGER PROUDLY SHARED
HE WEARS BOXER BRIEFS.
ADDING "THE COMBO PACKAGE" IS THE BEST PACKAGE TO
HOLD THE PACKAGE.
THANKS, NICK!

BACK TO YOU GUYS.

Yep, my job today is talking about a reality star's sex life, a
singer's onstage drama, and a pop star's private parts. If I am
indeed a "spiritual being" as Scientology asserts, it's evident
that I am not exhibiting this on the job every day in front of
millions of people. Christians might say I am not "glorifying
God," Hindus and Buddhists might observe that my actions
aren't aligned with the cosmic order of my dharma, and, from
what I can surmise, Scientologists might say I am not "pres-
ently realizing my unlimited capabilities."

When I unclip my mike from my tie and head to the bathroom to wipe the caked-on makeup from my face, I am feeling down, wondering how much longer I can dedicate myself
to something that feels more and more like a distraction from
my spiritual reality than a celebration of it. Perhaps this is the
perfect day for me to take a class on managing life's ups and
downs.

I arrive at the Scientology center on Sunset Boulevard a
few minutes early and find a parking spot in the otherwise
packed lot. The center is in a low-income neighborhood a
couple miles east of the polished bustle of tourism near the
intersection of Hollywood and Highland, with the building

just a few yards from the sidewalk. There are no barbed-wire fences, nothing imposing at all about the grounds. With its classical Greek columns on the facade and expansive lobby window, the blue building looks more like a modern library than a temple.

As I sit in my car munching on Chex Mix so that I don't pass out in the middle of my class, a security guard starts circling me on a bicycle, conspicuously eyeballing me as if I am a suspicious visitor in my Mercedes SUV.

Rather than cause any more consternation on my or his part, I exit my car and walk toward the front entrance. Its glass doors are propped open and visitors, all normal-looking enough, come and go. I step up to the front desk and tell the lady that I am here to take a class.

"Wonderful!" she says. "Welcome to Scientology."

The front desk clerk is tall, thin, attractive, and inviting. Not creepy whatsoever. However, she is wearing a white blouse and black slacks like the other uniformed workers I see stationed over in the bookstore across the glass-enclosed lobby, the tile floors of which are so shiny I could eat scrambled eggs off them and not fear illness. The uniforms are well tailored and stylish. The clerk slides a card across the counter and asks me to fill it out, but when I look at it I feel a little thrown.

"Oh, I already gave all my information when I signed up online for the class," I tell her.

She offers a customer-is-always-right smile. "We just want to make sure we have the correct information."

Though re-filling out my personal information seems redundant, I complete the short form and supply my name, address, and phone number—that is, my work address and phone number since I didn't want to give the church my personal ones.

"Great!" she says. "Tommy here will get you started."[1]

A tall, clean-cut guy in his twenties who had been hovering near the desk steps toward me.

"Hello, Ken," Tommy says, gripping my right hand with a firm, damn-glad-to-meet-ya shake. "I will take you back to the enrollment office."

"But I already enrolled online," I say.

"Yeah, we know," he says. "But we have to have you check in first."

I feel my face grow warm. My heart is beating faster.

"But I just want to take the class," I reply. "I don't want to enroll in any program."

Tommy explains that it's just normal procedure. I don't bother protesting. I've come here to take a class and I don't want to let their byzantine bureaucracy prevent me from doing that.

As Tommy leads me down the main hallway behind the front desk, I tell him I need to use the bathroom.

He detours us to a stairwell up to the second floor.

"Do people call you Kenny?" Tommy asks me randomly.

"My family does," I reply.

"Is your legal name Kenneth or Ken?"

"It's Kenneth," I say.

Tommy laughs. "That's pretty formal, huh?"

I give a "yep" as I follow him.

"So what do you do for a living?"

"I'm a writer," I say.

[1]   His name has been changed to respect his privacy.

"Oh, cool," Tommy says. "What kind of stuff do you write? Screenplays?"

"Well, I have dabbled in TV and movie scripts, but I write books—fiction and nonfiction."

"Well, you sound like L. Ron Hubbard," Tommy says gleefully. "He did both too."

As we awkwardly small talk down the hall I scan the walls, which are lined with photographs of members doing things like studying and attending church gatherings, and historical pictures of what appear to be leaders. Every twenty feet or so there are doors.

"Are these the classrooms?" I ask.

"Some of them," he answers, stopping in front of one door. "Here's the restroom. I will wait for you out here." That's good, because it would be creepy for him to monitor my restroom activity.

I thank him and enter the bathroom. After I pee, my cell phone chirps with a text alert on my way to the sink. I glance at it.

Hi Ken.

It is from a 323 number that I don't have in my contacts. Strange timing that I would get a text from an unknown number just as I am about to enroll in my Scientology class. But I just chalk it up to someone messing with me, seeing as though I spent all day telling people at work how nervous I was about coming here. A producer told me they might kidnap me. Another correspondent suggested I beware of them "love bombing" me, and another warned they would "brainwash" me. Obviously, despite being the only religion synonymous with

Hollywood, the staff of the leading news organization covering Hollywood is highly suspicious of it.

Tommy escorts me back downstairs into the enrollment office. A few women sit at cubicles at their computers in a setup
that reminds me of the sales department at a car dealership.
Tommy introduces me to one of the ladies, Angela[2], who offers me the customer's chair next to her desk and types on her
computer.

"So you signed up for the Ups and Downs class, correct?"
she asks.

"Yes, online. Like, last week."

"Perfect," Angela says all perky. "Did you get my text?"

"Excuse me?" I ask.

"I sent you a message a few minutes ago," she explains.
"You were late so I was making sure you were still coming."

*How did she get my cell phone number? Maybe I gave them my cell
on the application.*

"Oh," I reply, trying not to show my freaked-out-ness.

"Tommy will now show you the orientation video," she
explains. "It will give you an overview of Scientology."

Tommy, who has been lurking behind the desk, points me
to the video monitor outside the enrollment office in what's
called the Public Information Center, which is basically a
museum-like series of video monitors and printed displays. I
take a seat in front of the screen and he presses Play.

The video begins with dramatic orchestral music and beau-
tifully shot scenes of Scientologists at work and play. As images
flash on the screen, the narrator begins to explain the Scien-

---

[2]   Her name has been changed to respect her privacy.

tology view of the world. He says there are only two types of people in the world—those with a "social personality" and those with an "antisocial personality"—and that crimes and criminal acts are committed by "antisocials."

Images flash of war and violence and even a nuclear mushroom cloud as the narrator asserts that scientists have reigned over the most violent times in history as we have veered from our true nature. And then, later, I recall seeing the image of a scientist in a lab coat. He is stroking a monkey, but suddenly, the monkey leaps from his clutches and runs away. Conspicuously, there is no mention of Tom Cruise or any other celebrities.

The voice then explains, "The reason why we ride a roller coaster is suppression," which he says is done to us by "people intent to keep others down."

The narrator says that "artists are magnets for these kind of people." The music turns dour as images of sad musicians and actors and painters pop on the screen and he adds, "Dreams are mysteriously shattered."

According to the narrator, only 20 percent of the population are antisocials but "their havoc can be devastating."

The voice further explains their dualistic worldview:

- An antisocial has a bad sense of property
- But a social has respect
- A social person is eager to relay good news
- Antisocials do the complete opposite and they will not pass on good news
- The antisocial (or "AS") will alter communication to make it worse

"It's easy to spot who these suppressive people are," he says. "With these tools you can build a better life for yourselves and those around you."

After the short video ends, and I try to process the weirdness that I just witnessed, I walk back into the enrollment office.

"How did you like the video?" Tommy asks.

"It was *interesting*," I say diplomatically, not wanting to offend.

I sit back down at Angela's desk. As Tommy leans against the wall nearby within earshot, Angela slides some papers across the desk.

"Now, just sign this and you can start your class," she says.

I glance at the first page. At the top it reads "Religious Services Enrollment Application, Enrollment and Release." What follows are several paragraphs of dense legalese calling the document a "Contract." There is a clause stating I will never sue the church or its leaders.

"What is this for?" I ask.

"Just a standard waiver," she says.

I read further into the document, which goes from defining what Scientology is (a religion) but devolves by the end into very legalistic language about my waiving my right to make claims against the church or its leaders.

"Sorry, I can't sign this," I tell Angela, sliding the paperwork back to her.

"Why?" she asks, seeming shocked.

"I just don't sign any contracts without having a lawyer or someone look at it," I explain. "I'm in the entertainment industry, and this is pretty much standard, so I'm sure you can understand that."

"But don't you want to take the class?" she asks.

I feel Tommy's eyes focused on me from across the office.

"Yes, but I thought I would come here, take a class, and see what I could get out of it," I say. "I have been to many churches and spiritual gatherings and no one has ever asked me to sign anything. It just doesn't seem right."

Tommy steps in and subtly nods at Angela as they lock eyes. He takes over in their team sales tactic. "It totally makes sense that you might be reluctant to sign something," he says. "But you gotta understand that there are a lot of people out there who want to destroy Scientology and that we have to protect ourselves."

"I understand," I say firmly, feeling sales-force pressure. "But you have to understand that I just don't sign contracts without consulting a lawyer."

I take hold of the contract. "Look, I will gladly take this to my lawyer, sign it and bring it back so I can take the class."

"Sorry, but we don't allow that," Angela says.

Now I am not only growing anxious, but I am very annoyed. I feel as if they are treating me like an idiot.

"I just want to take a class," I say.

"But we can't let you up into the classroom if you don't sign this," she says. "It's just our policy."

I shrug and as I am about to get up and leave, Angela looks to Tommy. He asks me to come with him. Reluctantly, I do, following him to a small room at the end of the office. Inside, there are two chairs facing each other. Tommy closes the door and sits beside me.

"Ken, I really want you to take this class. When I first joined, this was my first class. It helped me tremendously. At the time, man, I was doing drugs and in a real bad place, but that class helped me." Tommy leans forward so close I can smell his breath mint. "And even though I don't know what you are struggling with, I know that whatever it is, it will help you."

I cross my legs and nod.

He continues, "Is there anything you are struggling with?"

"What do you mean?"

"Well, you signed up for this class," he says, sitting back. "So I assume there is some reason you signed up."

Now I'm feeling probed, that my intelligence is being insulted, and I am no longer comfortable.

"Look, Tommy, I don't want to offend you," I say. "You seem like a real nice guy, and I am so glad that you have overcome your issues with the help of Scientology. But I just came here to take a class. If I have to sign a contract just to take a class, that's just not gonna happen. I am sure you understand."

"Oh, completely," he says.

"So maybe I can buy a couple books, learn more about Scientology, and when I am comfortable, maybe I will come back and sign it," I reason.

"I know in all my heart," Tommy adds, hand on chest, "that Scientology will help lead you to a trail to a better life, like it did for me. You will not regret it."

"I appreciate your caring, but—"

"So let's do this," Tommy interrupts, standing up. "We will have you meet with our librarian. So sit tight and I will go get her and she can walk you through."

"But can't I just go to the bookstore?" I ask. "I saw it up front when I came in."

"Of course, but I think it's best if she is able to show you personally the books." Yeah, I think, best for *you* to keep me

caged here like a tough-bargaining customer at Toyota of Tor-
rance haggling over whether to buy a Prius.

After Tommy leaves, I close my eyes and take a deep breath
in and let it out, just as I have been doing with my daily meditations. I am feeling anxious and my heart rate is high. Several
breaths later, I begin to settle down. Still, while I am turned
off by their tactics, I am also conflicted about what to do next.
Part of me wants to run out while I am still alive and my brain
is unwashed, while the other part of me wants to see which
wacky pressure-sales tactic they will throw at me next.

As I sit waiting for Tommy to come back with the "librarian," I scope the walls of the meeting room.

On one hangs a sign reading, THE ONLY RICHNESS THERE IS,
IS UNDERSTANDING. THAT IS ALL THAT SCIENTOLOGY HAS TO
GIVE. —LRH

And another poster shows a volcano erupting with the slogan, YOUR ADVENTURE HAS ONLY JUST BEGUN . . . They sure
do seem obsessed with cataclysm, war, and "Us vs. Them"
disaster messaging.

Tommy returns a few minutes later with another tall, thin
white woman clutching a stack of books. She goes through
each of them, starting with *Dianetics*, which she calls "the
original" by founder L. Ron Hubbard and is described as "the
bestselling book on the human mind." In a paperback edition
for *Dianetics*, in the praise-quotes section at the beginning is
an endorsement from John Travolta: "*Dianetics* put me into the
big time. I always had the ability to be somewhat successful,
but *Dianetics* freed me up to the point where something really
big could happen, without interference."

A dozen or so books later, totaling over $200, she asks me
which ones I want. I pick *Dianetics* and *The Way to Happiness*

by Hubbard, and another one titled *Scientology: A New Slant on Life*, also written by Hubbard. "I'll get started with these and go from there," I tell her.

Angela rings me up and as I am about to pay with my credit card, she goes, "You know, there is an option for you to take classes from home. It is our extension course. And the great thing about it is that you can take the first class upstairs."

My ears perk. "So I *can* go upstairs?" I ask.

"Yes, but only for the first class," she says, totally reversing what she had insisted was a strict policy that I must first sign a contract. "The course is based off the *New Slant* book." She slides a gray-and-green laminated workbook over to me. "With this and the book you can take the class."

I don't call her out. I have gotten what I wanted. But I do ask, "Haven't I missed the start time of the class, though?"

"It is self-guided, but there is a teacher there to help you," she explains.

After I pay for the books and the extension course (totaling $110.67), Tommy shakes my hand and, with a toothy smile, thanks me for coming. A testament to Tommy's likability and charm is that, even though I felt pressured and insulted by his recruiting tactics, I actually feel kind of bad for turning him down. Damn, he's good!

Nonetheless, I grab my bag of books and follow Angela up to the second-floor classroom.

A Latina woman greets us inside and Angela hands her my course booklet.

The room looks like any other classroom, with individual desks lined up in a row. There are a half dozen people, including a teenager, sitting and reading and writing with a pen into workbooks. The teenager gets up and walks robotically to a shelf and returns a book, then leaves the room in a militaristic march step. In fact, the only thing about the classroom that suggests I am in a Scientology study center is I see an E-meter on a table at the front of the class.

The teacher opens up the class workbook and, in a gentle voice with a strong accent, explains there are no wrong answers and the only key is to be honest with each question. She says that for future classes I can just fill out the workbooks and mail them in or drop them off here. But for now, I just need to read the introduction of *New Slant* and a chapter titled "Is It Possible to Be Happy?" and then fill out the questions in the workbook.

"But why can't I just take the classes online?"

Her answer: "We don't do it that way."

My actress friend was right. These people are very nice. But now that I am experiencing their recruitment tactics, I also conclude they are very manipulative.

Though miffed, I sit down and open the book and begin reading Hubbard's introduction, which concludes with, "What are your goals? Where are you going? Why are you here? What *are* you? Scientology has answers to these questions, good answers that are true, answers that will work for you. For the subject matter of Scientology is *you*."

I flip to the first chapter on happiness and read that "the truth of the matter is that all the happiness you will ever find lies in *you*." The chapter is essentially a very engaging essay on how the world can distract us in ways that lead to unhappiness, but that being in touch with our true spirit, our eternal energy, knowing our true self, is the key to finding happiness. It is the most I have ever read of Hubbard's writings and I am struck by the clarity, simplicity, and confidence of the prose.

And I don't disagree with much of what he has observed about the epidemic of unhappiness in the world, which, in truth, I have fallen into.

But when I read the final line of the chapter, Hubbard loses me when he writes that the thing that makes it possible for man to know himself is: Scientology. What about meditation? What about prayer? What about psychotherapy? What about belief in any of the other faith traditions? As I am finding over and over in my search for God, the claim of being the exclusive path to enlightenment comes across as intellectually dishonest and self-serving.

I turn to the workbook and thumb through the 104 questions I am to answer after reading the entire book. Some are personal (Give an example of a time when you trusted your own observations and had the courage to say so . . .) and others are typical questions with answers that can be lifted right from the book. But my gut tells me not to write down my answers and turn them over to the church. What if they get angry at me, what if they don't like what I may say or write about them in the future? Might they use my "case file" against me like they have reportedly done to Leah Remini and other critics? My albeit cursory investigation into Tom Cruise-ology has led me to believe it's not that I don't trust the philosophies and self-improvement practices of Scientology, because there definitely seems to be merit in Hubbard's view of the human mind and ways to heal it on a spiritual level. So why do I close my workbook without answering a single question in it, grab my book bag, and walk out of the room? Because I don't trust the messengers, the late Hubbard's neo-minions who are administering his vision. Not from what I have read, or from what I have seen on TV, or have been told by friends. My repulsed feelings come from spending two hours being cajoled, seemingly misled, pressured, and sold on a spiritual practice. Call me crazy, but I don't want my introduction to a spiritual practice to feel like I have stepped inside a boiler room. Their behavior—tracking me down via text messaging, running me through several layers of car dealer–like salesmanship, telling me I could not go into the classroom without signing a legally binding contract only to reverse their stance and invite me into a classroom in which I am expected to reveal personal secrets and demons on paperwork that, according to the contract, the church has the legal right to possess and do whatever they want with—makes me feel like the whole recruitment is about them, not me. No thanks. If there is a God in Hollywood—and I truly believe there is—I would rather not find Him at all than do so at the expense of my own dignity and personal boundaries.

I hustle outside the room before the teacher can stop me, to find Angela standing outside the door. "You're leaving?" she asks with a confused stare.

"Yeah, I'm sorry, but I've been here for almost two hours and I am tired and have a long commute back home," I lie. "Thanks for letting me take the class. But I am going to leave now."

I leave Angela, mouth agape, at her post outside the classroom, walk quickly downstairs, and exit the building knowing I will never come back to the Church of Scientology of Los Angeles—no matter how much I love Tom Cruise movies.

XIV

LISTEN TO THE "FIELD OF DREAMS"

I get home from my visit to Scientology and, after changing my shirt because I had sweated so much during my visit, I tell Brooke and the kids about the unnerving experience that happened to me from simply trying to take a class. Jackson and Chloe can't believe how much they pressured me and harassed me to sign a contract.

"Not gonna lie, guys," I regale them at the dinner table. "I was more nervous sitting in that office than I am sitting in front of a camera with millions of people watching."

"Are they mad at you?" Chloe asks with worry.

"I don't think so," I reply. "But they would probably have been happier if I signed up."

"I am scared," she says. "They might come after you."

I assure Chloe that she doesn't need to worry about anyone coming after me or her. But my eleven-year-old girl's concern is clearly feeding off the anxiety I am emitting about my experience.

Then Jackson asks, "What religion are we?"

"I was raised Catholic, but I don't have one I can say I belong to," I reply. "Do you believe in one?"

"I don't know," Jackson says with a shrug. "Not Scientology."

Neither of my kids knows what religion they are, because they haven't been taught by me or Brooke to follow any particular tradition. Neither of us wanted to push any religious agenda on them and early on agreed to expose them to different religions. They've attended Jewish services, gone to a few Easter and Christmas church services, meditated at yoga classes and chanted in Sanskrit, and they have heard their grandfather preach about the Bible on occasion.

"Well, I am sort of in the same boat as you," I reveal to Jackson. "That's why I am on my search to find answers, because I want to know what I believe. You can do the same, you know. You can explore other faiths and research them. You'll start figuring it out for yourself."

Four months later in August, Jackson and I are on a trip alone to Iowa. He has been invited to attend a weeklong hockey camp in the city of Waterloo, an old mill town in the northeastern part of the state near the Minnesota border.

Thinking it would be neat to watch a movie that took place in Iowa, I download *Field of Dreams* on my iPad and on our first night in the hotel room Jackson and I watch the 1989 movie starring Kevin Costner. In addition to capturing the rural beauty of Iowa in the summer, *Field of Dreams*, about a financially strapped farmer (Costner) who hears voices telling him to build a baseball diamond in his backyard, is also a tear-jerking father/son story. After building the diamond amid a field of corn, ghosts dressed as baseball players come and play. In a very touching closing scene, Costner realizes that one of the players—spoiler alert!—is his late father, who died brokenhearted from never realizing his dream of playing pro baseball. The scene, poignantly showing that sometimes we are led to do things by a higher power though we may not know why, has me in tears, which I try to conceal from Jackson with a sly wipe of my cheek with my sleeve as Costner's dad looks around the field and asks, "Is this heaven?" To which he replies, "It's Iowa."

The next day after Jackson's morning practice, I meet him beside our rental car outside the ice arena.

"How was practice, buddy?"

"Good."

"I have an idea for something fun to do," I say.

"I don't want to go bowling," Jackson moans. I had earlier suggested a bowling trip for us since we saw an alley nearby. "I hate bowling."

"My idea is way better than that," I say. "Let's go to the real Field of Dreams."

His eyes light up. "The one in the movie?"

"Yeah! I looked it up and the real place—the baseball field, the farm, the house, everything—is still there. And it's only an hour's drive from here."

"Cool," he says. "Are you sure it's open?"

"Yep," I say, smugly. "I checked, and it is open today. And it's free. You can go on the field and play and just soak it all in."

And an hour later, we get off Highway 20 and snake our way through a narrow rural road up a hill and around a bend. At the top, I turn my Honda rental car right, and a few hundred yards ahead we can see the white farmhouse up the road, surrounded by a picket fence, with the baseball field to the left.

I hang a left onto the gravel driveway and park in the lot

right behind home plate. There are no other cars in the parking lot, except for one next to the gift shop that is probably the shop worker's sedan. It is a Monday afternoon in early August in eastern Iowa. My Google map says we are 204 miles from Chicago, 190 miles from Des Moines and 237 miles from Minneapolis. But taking in the vast blue sky dotted with clouds scraped above a lush green vista of cornfields it looks to me like we are, as observed by the ball player in the movie, in heaven.

Jackson runs from the car toward the baseball field. When he gets to the bench next to the fence backstop he finds a pile of bats and balls and gloves.

"Are you sure this is free?" he asks me excitedly.

"Totally," I say. "Let's play."

For the next half hour we run the bases, play catch, and I pitch him balls that he hits into the outfield, rounding the bases for home runs. Jackson is a hockey player, and only played one season of tee-ball, but you'd think he was Major League.

When he tires out, we leave the equipment near home plate and walk to the edge of the cornfield that rings the outfield. I take some video of Jackson walking into the cornfield, disappearing just as the ghosts did in the movie.

"Oh, my God!" he yells from inside the dense thicket of corn.

I run into the field and find Jackson, an L.A. kid with little experience in nature, bent over staring at the ground.

"I found a frog!" he says.

"Have you ever seen a frog?" I ask.

"Not in real life," he confesses. "This is cool."

We fight our way through the tall corn and lie down in the outfield grass, staring up at the sky.

I sigh. "Remember the time you asked me what religion I believe?"

"Uh-huh," he replies.

"And you told me that you didn't know what you believed in, and I said to research it and you may find some answers. So, have you done that?"

"Yeah," Jackson says. "I have."

"And . . . ?"

"OK, dad. Here's the thing." Jackson sits up. "I seventy percent believe there's a God. But I think there are just some things in life that are unexplainable. There is a lot of complicated stuff that we can't answer."

All those YouTube videos he watches constantly must be educating my towheaded teen more than I thought.

Jackson goes on. "Here's what I believe is reality. There are many universes, not just one. It's string theory. Universes can split apart and connect. The Big Bang was, like, the connecting of universes, not just the creation of one. You know what I am saying?"

"I think so, yeah. But go on."

"So, yeah," he says. "I think that the whole question of the universe and how it came about is very complicated and we'll never be able to explain it."

"OK, but who do you think created these universes?" I ask.

"Or maybe it's more like *what* created it," he answers. "We don't know what created everything, which is why I don't think I am a Christian or Jewish or anything like that. Because if God is real, then I don't think it could just be one. That seems very close-minded to me."

"So you can't believe in any one religion."

"Right. Everyone needs to stop worrying about who created all this and just accept that it's unexplainable and we are
meant just to live. You know what I think? I think these ancient people came up with the idea of a higher power to explain it, but, really, it is just a theory that hasn't been proved
and there are many other theories out there to investigate as
we learn more information about science." He pauses, then
adds, "And stuff like that."

I laugh. Not at all because what he is saying is funny, but
because it is so brilliant and insightful, especially for a kid who
just became a teenager five months ago.

"I saw this video," Jackson continues, "and they said in it
that Elon Musk thinks that there is an eighty percent chance
we are in a computer simulation. It's infinite."

I sit up and we face each other on the grass. The breeze is
warm and gentle. The air is clean and, for the first time since
I began my spiritual quest, I feel totally at peace, as if I am
one with nature or God or the universe or . . . whatever it is
that Jackson is so eloquently describing is our physical reality.
I don't feel like just asking questions and listening to Jackson
is bringing me closer to that elusive God I so badly want to
know. I'm realizing that just the simple process of asking and
listening is the most direct path to a higher power, that having
an open mind and open heart is what's been allowing answers
to come to me, just as the voice of God told Kevin Costner,
"If you build it, he will come."

Since Jackson seems to have given these deep, spiritual questions a lot of careful consideration in between playing video
games and stopping pucks, I throw another doozy at him.

"Jackson, you know how *Field of Dreams* is so much about

following your dreams, and about listening to that voice inside of you? I'm wondering what your dream is."

Jackson stares off toward the green vista. After a good ten seconds, he goes, "I don't know, but it's definitely to do something cool with my life."

Amen to that.

XV

FIND SOME HEADSPACE

Don't let the sound of your own wheels drive you crazy . . .
—THE EAGLES, "TAKE IT EASY"

A breakthrough: Ask and listen. I don't have to be sitting in the middle of Iowa on location of a classic Hollywood movie to practice this spiritual act.

Before I am even back in Los Angeles, I decide to approach my spiritual journey as a listening campaign more than a seeking expedition. On the flight from Iowa, I listen to a series of guided meditations on my Headspace app led by the soothing voice of Andy, the bald Buddhist monk who has become my virtual guru.

I have been practicing these ten-minute, Zen-inspired meditations with him for a few months now, every day, and I have noticed that I am more relaxed, more focused, and less anxious and distracted. I feel more . . . centered. It didn't happen overnight; there wasn't a single moment when it hit me like, "Hey, this meditation shit is working!" Rather, I have just been consistent in closing my eyes, calming my breath, and training my mind to be still and when it wanders into my worry place, bring my focus back to the breath. At first, the ten minutes seemed like ten hours. Now, though, it goes by so fast I often just keep meditating past when the bell rings.

Somewhere over Nebraska, I click on the "Happiness" series, which begins with Andy explaining in a short video tutorial the meditation tool of visualization.

"Anybody can learn to visualize," he says. "Imagine a friend or family member, or someone you really like; just bring them to mind for a moment."

He pauses. I choose to picture the guy seated next to me: my son, Jackson.

Andy explains that when our mind gets distracted, we need not panic or have an emotional reaction to losing our focus. Instead, he suggests, we just "gently" bring our mind back to the breath or the mental image. Over time, he says, the mind will soften and more easily focus on the moment.

I then click on Day One of the "Happiness" meditation and begin.

Andy starts with an explanation of what his Buddhism-informed definition of happiness is, saying a regular practice may not make you laugh and smile more but rather bring "an underlying fulfillment, contentment and satisfaction in our life."

My meditation starts with Andy encouraging me to maintain a soft focus ahead and as I gaze gently to get comfortable in my seat I breathe in through my nose and out through my mouth, settling myself down. Self-soothing until I am feeling calm—something I needed a Xanax to do just a few months ago.

Then I close my eyes and let my breath find its natural rhythm and become aware of my body, feel it pressed against the airplane seat, my feet placed on the cabin floor and hands rested on my thighs.

Andy gently instructs me to scan from head to toe and "check in" with my physical self, noting how it feels—getting a sense along the way for "the general mood for the mind."

Then Andy urges me to take a moment to be clear about why I am doing this happiness exercise, and I think about how I am doing this because I hope to learn how to be as happy every day as I was on that Field of Dreams with Jackson.

He tells me to notice the rising and falling sensation of my breath and, when I do, I feel like I am floating, like any tenseness or worry is drifting away from my body, as if I am hypnotized yet totally self-aware at the same time.

My breath is now slow and effortless. Then, I do as he suggests and imagine a pinprick of light in the middle of my chest, representing all the happiness I seek in my life, and I visualize it getting bigger and bigger until the light fills my entire body.

As I picture this lightness of being overtaking me, I feel completely at rest, entirely fulfilled in the moment. I am present. Before I know it, the ten minutes is up and Andy is telling me to gently open my eyes. And as I take in the packed airplane, an environment that once made me feel agitated and claustrophobic, I feel very . . . well, happy. As my son and I speed over the majestic Rockies at five hundred miles an hour, I feel more still than I ever have. And I wonder if my blissful state of just being *me* is actually the state of being one with God.

XVI

QUESTION THE GOSPEL ACCORDING TO KANYE WEST

As a student at the Columbia Graduate School of Journalism, professors taught me that the key to conducting an effective interview wasn't just asking questions, but also listening closely to the answers.

Throughout my search for God, my busy brain has always been filled with questions—*How do I know that God is real? Which religion is the truest? What happens when I die? Do I believe in heaven? Can the Bible be believed?*—and my seeking answers to these questions has been the fuel driving me forward on my freeway to faith.

But for me to ask questions without listening—to others and myself—would be like driving down that highway with a blindfold, missing an opportunity to enjoy what's passing by and risking major personal injury. So I have been trying to pay more attention to everything and everyone around me, being more mindfully aware of the moment, tapping into the divine power of listening, and just being in the moment. It may sound very New Age–y and *Power of Now*–y, but living mindfully like this has taken a profound hold on me.

When I meditate—and I have done Headspace series on Creativity, Relationships, Stress, Anxiety, Happiness, and Focus—I have gotten to know my inner self more intimately and in that calmness I have had moments where I didn't think, I didn't feel, I was just being. By turning off my brain—really, losing my mind—I am finding I am less confused about what I believe. I am going clear—and I didn't need Scientology to do it. I just needed to be mindful.

Yet I still have many questions about who God is and how to know this supreme creator and exactly what my relationship is to it. Of course, I could say, "Ken, just chill out and stop thinking. You've already found God—within!" But while I would like to fancy myself a full-time meditating monk, I am not quite that advanced on my spiritual journey. Intellectually, I have some loose ends. And perhaps the loosest one remaining is the one that dates back the furthest into my spiritual life: the Jesus Question.

Ever since attending Easter services with Pastor Brad and the Kardashians, I have been wanting to talk privately with Brad. We have tried many times to connect in person, but invariably bad L.A. traffic, or conflicting schedules, torpedoed our plans. So today I closed my office door, sat down, and called the peppy pastor.

After some small talk, I get right to the heart of what's been most on my mind.

"I am really struck by your conviction of how much you believe in Jesus and how passionate you are about sharing your faith," I tell him. "It really is beautiful and inspiring, to be honest. But I'm just not there, I don't think."

"Where are you trying to go?" Brad asks.

"I guess I'm trying to believe in the God you believe in," I say. "But how do you, intellectually, take what the Bible teaches and the stories in it so literally? Because I have serious doubts. Do you really believe in all your heart and soul and mind that, without a doubt, the God in the Bible is the one, true God?"

"I really do have a belief that there is a singular, personal God, and He is revealed to us in the Bible," Brad says. "The reason for that is Jesus. Up until the coming of the Messiah, which represents all of the Jewish faith, there was this impersonal, distant Me-Thou God. Then Jesus said, "When you have seen me you have seen the father. Jesus was described as the word that became flesh. And he lived with us. For me it is the idea of God wanting to be more than vague and more than a concept and more than distant. He really wants us to know him personally. Not just an idea, but personally. Ideas become opinions, but Jesus wanted us to see fact. To see how to live. And Jesus lived exactly what he promised and delivered."

"I respect that, but why should I believe Jesus just because he says it's true?" I ask. "I mean, Kanye West likes to say he's the best, and calls himself 'Yeezus' as if he is a messiah, but a lot of people don't take him seriously."

Brad laughs. "It's a good question. There is a book called *The Case for Christ*. The author reminds me a little of you, because it seems like you want to assemble evidence to help you make a decision. The author is this guy named Lee Strobel; he was a journalist for *The Chicago Tribune* and a real cynical skeptic. He had a sign in his office that read, 'If your mother says "I love you," check your sources.' In terms of faith, he was a card-carrying atheist. He had even donated money to the American Association of Atheists. He had an ID card. But his wife began to follow Jesus and he was struck by the changes he saw in her life.

"So he went and investigated all the claims Jesus made, analyzed all the stories and compared them to what we know of the historical record. He went one by one through all the events that were prophesied hundreds of years before they came true—from a baby being born in Bethlehem to the crucifixion to the resurrection—dozens of promises about the Messiah. He did this with the intention of debunking all these stories as myths. After he researched it all, and found that, incredibly, they were accurate, he went to a mathematician and asked him what the odds were of the Bible predicting so many events, and the professor said there is a greater likelihood that a tornado could rush through a junkyard and assemble a 747."

"Sounds like a David Blaine magic act," I joke.

"Remarkable, right?" Brad says. "The Gospels are eye-witness accounts and give testimony to all these miraculous things. Just think about this: Five hundred people gave testimony of having seen Jesus alive and walking and talking after he had been executed and buried. So even the evidence for the resurrection is compelling and overwhelming. Now, cynics and Doubting Thomases might say, 'I want to see five hundred and one sources!' But it is compelling enough to me to conclude that, yes, the Bible is the real deal. So we must conclude one of three things about Jesus: (1) He is a liar, like David Koresh or Sun Myung Moon or some other cult leader, or (2) He is a lunatic, meaning he believes what he is saying but his perception is very warped, or (3) He is the Lord and exactly who he claimed himself to be."

I almost ask whether Jesus could have been all three things—a liar, a lunatic, and the Lord—but I stop myself because it seems disrespectful and not in the spirit of my newfound "listening campaign."

Brad continues, "If you take the weight of evidence, I will stake my claim on the side of believing that he is God's son and I should give my life to following him.

"I remember reading once something along the lines of, 'If I am wrong, and I die and there is no heaven, then I had nothing to lose. But if I'm right, I have everything to gain.' So there really isn't a downside in trusting and believing in Christ."

That logic is exactly why my dad prayed with my brother Kevin a few months before he died and accepted Jesus Christ as the Lord. He was hedging his bets.

"So, in other words, he who loves Vegas should love Christ?" I joke.

Brad has a very good sense of humor and as such laughs pretty hard. "Well," he says, "I think the evidence of Jesus is greater than the Vegas odds."

"Brad, the truth is that I'm getting the sense that I am not going to think my way into believing anything," I say. "I am concluding that, ultimately, I need to feel my way to the truth."

"Well, my friend," Brad says. "God wants you to know Him. He is there. You just need to listen to your heart."

"I've been trying to do that, actually," I tell him. "I have been meditating every day, sometimes twice a day. And it's really helped me get in touch with my inner self, my inner voice."

"And what is it saying?" he asks.

"Keep meditating."

"Then do that," he says. "Meditation and prayer can be one in the same. It can be divine."

XVII

EVEN JESUS SHALL NEED A PUBLICIST

Christianity is the religion of my youth, the predominant faith in our culture—and the entire world, with about one-third of the world's population (over 2.2 billion people) identifying themselves as Christian (Islam ranks second, with 1.6 billion followers).

I don't feel drawn to Islam, probably because I don't connect with its cultural trappings—and the same could be said for Judaism and other spiritual practices. But for me, an Irish Catholic boy from suburban Buffalo, Christianity is not easily dismissed.

Of course, popularity doesn't necessarily make a religion the optimal path to finding God, or, say, the quickest path to enlightenment. To put it in Hollywood terms, One Direction might have been a really popular singing group, but they had cheesy songs and eventually broke up and everyone moved on. Ditto, Every-Boy-Band *Ever*.

So does Christianity's enduring popularity stem from its inspiring message of eternal salvation through faith in Christ?

Or did Jesus just have a really good team of publicists in the form of his disciples?

If I have learned anything in Hollywood, no matter how good your product might be it will fail if no one knows about it. And no matter how good your marketing and publicity efforts, if your product truly sucks, then people won't consume it over the long term. In that sense, there is something to be said for the lasting predominance of all the great world religions, including Christianity.

If Christianity is the most popular American religion, then one of its most visible preachers (and a very media-savvy publicist for Jesus) is the Rev. Joel Osteen. I have long been a fan of Osteen's preaching style and his uplifting message. For years, even the ones where I was not spending any serious time contemplating my faith, I would stumble upon his TV sermons on Sunday mornings from his Lakewood megachurch in Houston. His messages are inspiring and positive. He's what I would call a motivational preacher, something of a latter-day Norman Vincent Peale, who was known for his 1950s bestselling book *The Power of Positive Thinking*. In fact, there is often very little difference between Osteen's messages and those of a secular motivational speaker—except that, naturally, he always ties in that faith in Jesus is what makes all things possible. Otherwise, it is his aw-shucks genuineness and overall positivity (without any of the sliminess of televangelists of yore) served on a massive TV and book platform that has made him arguably the most popular preacher today. Sure, he has come under criticism from all sides for either being too watered-down or making millions off his publishing and TV empire, which reaches 100 million households, but I still enjoy listening to him, critics be damned.

Having grown up in an era when televangelist scandals were as common as formulaic *Rocky* films, I do have a reasonable dose of skepticism around virtuous preachers who use television to reach the masses while also building massive fundraising machines.

There was Jimmy Swaggart, the Bible-shaming Southern minister caught having sex with a prostitute back in 1988, the year I graduated high school. A year earlier, another TV preaching star was Jim Bakker, who was busted having sex with a woman named Jessica Hahn and had paid her supposed "hush money" with church funds. Christian leader Jerry Falwell famously called Bakker "the greatest scab and cancer on the face of Christianity in 2,000 years of church history." Literally that same year, the "faith healer" Peter Popoff, who was reportedly making $4 million per year allegedly healing people of various ailments, was exposed as a fraud. Popoff would claim to heal people of cancer by simply yelling, "Back off, Devil!" and pressing his palm into their foreheads. The preacher with the shock of slicked-back black hair would call out people's names and their afflictions, without having met them, claiming that God was sending him the information so he could heal them. The scam was working until magician James Randi infiltrated Popoff's scheme and, with the help of a radio scanner, discovered that Popoff was being fed information not from God, but his wife (who had lifted the personal info from cards filled out by seekers ahead of time). These and other unsavory televangelistic characters damaged the credibility and image of all television preachers, while emboldening secular humanists and skeptics who have long criticized faith as mere fantasy.

But Joel Osteen represents the new generation. Sure, he asks for money, but it is a soft sell and his charities seem straight-forward about the work they do with donations. Sure, he has perfect teeth and a smile as bright as snow but he also preaches with humility and humor and a nonjudgmental tone.

When I saw recently during one of his Sunday TV shows an ad that he was coming to the Los Angeles area—specifically the Citizens Business Bank Arena in suburban Ontario—for one of his "Night of Hope" revivals I immediately got tickets. I may not be all in for Jesus, but when it comes to hearing inspiring messages of hope and faith and love, I am always open for business. His uplifting sermons, with titles such as "If You Believe, All Things Are Possible," focus on the transformative power of faith. Now I want to see him in person.

It's a Friday night, and I am driving east on the car-clogged I-10 freeway toward Ontario. Seated beside me is Trish, an *E! News* producer whom I have invited along because we often talk about religion in between taping sessions (she attends a church in L.A. every Sunday). Earlier, I emailed Joel's publicist (yes, even celebrity preachers need a PR rep) and she agreed to take me backstage after tonight's event for a quick "meet and greet," something I am very familiar with from my experiences with Taylor Swift or Justin Bieber concerts, but never with a spiritual leader.

Hungry, Trish and I hit the snack bar. When I pay for our chili dogs, popcorn, and water, the clerk hands me my credit card and says, "Enjoy the show!"

A show, indeed. When we leave the concourse and walk down the aisle, the 11,000-seat arena is close to sold out, packed with fans of his work such as me and local church groups showing up by the busloads to hear Joel and his wife, Victoria, backed by a soft-rock band, deliver their "message of hope" for the next two hours. The event, which very much feels like a concert, is also being broadcast live on Sirius XM Radio.

Trish and I are seated in the second row, directly behind Joel's eighty-three-year-old mom, a thin woman from Texas with big hair to prove it. After an upbeat introduction from the attractive band (cymbal clash! guitar solo! thumping bass!), Joel charges out onstage in his perfectly tailored blue suit and shiny black shoes, a smile as wide as the Texas Panhandle.

Joel strides across the stage and back again, both his hands free to gesticulate due to the presence of a tiny mike clipped to his jacket, thanking the crowd, most of whom are on their feet (including me), for coming to the Night of Hope.

"God can turn things around in a split second," Joel says, beaming. "God's going to accelerate your dreams and bring things to pass sooner than expected. Let tonight be a new beginning for your life."

He introduces his attractive, blond wife, Victoria, who bounds onto the stage and holds hands with Joel. Their stagecraft scores a little high on the Hilary Clinton Stiffness Scale. Even so, I find that I am smiling and genuinely like them.

"Maybe tonight you need to take off a coat of heaviness, a coat of discouragement, a coat of self-pity," Joel tells his congregation. "Take off that old coat and put on a coat of praise, of thanksgiving, of gratefulness to God." The crowd applauds, the first of dozens of palm-slapping breaks of praise.

Over the next two hours, between interludes of Christian rock, follows a Bible-based pump-up session that reminds me of when a speaker comes to a corporate retreat to fire up the troops, or a Tony Robbins seminar.

After a long week of work at *E! News* in which I got paid

to gossip about reality stars and sex-crazed socialites, Joel's aphorisms of positivity and hope make me feel like this spiritual journey I've been on for the better part of the last year is something I want to spend tonight celebrating. I decide I'm not going to judge Joel and sit here and intellectualize the influence his celebrity-like image and star quality is having on this crowd. I am not going to let my inner voice interfere with having a fun, innocent night of uplifting words from a guy who helps a lot of people feel less alone, less isolated, and more hopeful. His message manages to be based in scripture while not being of the offensive "follow Jesus or go to hell" variety. So as I settle in my seat I take a vow: Rather than question, analyze, and dissect, I will listen, absorb, and receive.

Which is easy to do when every other line out of Joel's mouth is something worth taping on my bathroom mirror:

"Happiness is a choice we make each day."

"Seeds of discouragement cannot take root in a grateful heart."

"Find something to be grateful for."

"Don't bring negative baggage from yesterday into today."

"Let every day be a new beginning."

"He's not just the God of perfect people, he is the God of imperfect people too."

"You wouldn't be alive unless God had another victory up in front of you."

"Let tonight be a new beginning in your life."

"You can feel good about who you are knowing that God picked you and put seeds of greatness on the inside."

"You don't need someone else's applause. I would rather have God's applause than people's applause."

"A promotion doesn't come from people, it comes from the Lord."

"Life goes better when you put God in first place."

"The forces that are for you are greater than the forces that are against you."

The energy of Joel's night has been building up to this: a guitar-backed crescendo of feel-good adjectives—"Lord, we are blessed, we are prosperous, we are redeemed, forgiven, talented, creative, confident, secure, prepared, qualified, motivated, equipped, empowered, anointed, accepted, and approved!" The band turns it up. "In Jesus's name!"

Joel slows it down. "Quit fighting it, quit trying to make everything work out your way, and just release control. Let those winds blow you to where God wants you to go. When you release control, quit worrying and losing sleep, and say, 'God, I trust you.'"

Then comes the "call to action" that happens at the end of every Christian revival. Joel asks us to bow our heads and softens his voice, imploring anyone who "needs a fresh, new start, or new beginning, to take the step of faith and stand where you are." I sneak a glance around the arena and see hundreds of people—young and old, of all races and ethnicities—getting to their feet, many raising their hands as if giving heaven a high-five. It's a heartwarming sight to see so many people showing their spiritual hunger in such a public, vulnerable way. But I am not among them. I have received and appreciated his message, and I am buoyed by his words.

"C'mon, Ontario!" Joel exults. "Let's give them a hand clap!"

The congregation obliges the joyous leader.

"The angels are rejoicing in heaven right now. It is gonna be a new beginning in your life. Let us pray, Lord, Jesus, I repent of my sins. Come into my heart. Wash me clean. I'll make you my Lord and savior." Joel looks up and smiles. "If you stood up, you are starting with a fresh, clean slate!"

After Joel leaves the stage, Joel's publicist comes to get me and Trish. She escorts us back to a VIP room underneath the seats. As we wait for Joel, I joke to Trish that VIP stands for "Very Important Pray-ers." Trish, embarrassed that I said it so loud among the other fans, elbows me in the ribs. "Ken! Shush!"

"What did you think?" I ask Trish, who, unlike me, is a regular churchgoer and self-described Christian.

"I loved it," she says. "He's a really gifted speaker. Thanks for inviting me."

Trish tilts her head. "And what did you think?"

I tilt my head in kind. "Well, I think this is exactly what I needed to do tonight. I am exactly where I am supposed to be."

"That's so Zen of you," she says.

I nod.

Joel walks in with his wife and starts shaking hands and

greeting the other VIPs. Eventually, he gets to me. He firmly shakes my hand. "I know who you are!" he enthuses.

"Do you watch E!?" I'm taken aback that a TV preacher watches the cable network of the flamboyant Kardashians and bitchy *Fashion Police* squad.

"I believe I do," says Joel, whom I notice is wearing as much makeup as I do for my work. "I recognize you. I do, I do. Good job!"

"Shouldn't you be reading the Bible instead?" I joke.

"Maybe, maybe," Joel says, adding, "but we all need a little break every now and then."

I convince Trish to take a quick picture on her phone of Joel posing with me. After, I lean in to Joel and tell him over the VIP room chatter, "You know, in my line of work, people come up to me and say, 'I'm a fan.' But I wanted to tell you that I am a *receiver* of yours. I am a receiver of your gifts."

He smiles and graciously replies, "I like that, thank you. Well said. God bless."

I didn't accept Jesus tonight. But I leave the arena having accepted what I believe is a greater truth: That I can appreciate and receive benefits from a message based on a faith in which I do not exclusively or entirely believe. I no longer need to stress about having to be entirely committed to a faith tradition in order to reap some wisdom and peace from it. If I am listening, learning, and doing so with the intention of hope, love, and insight, then I am living in faith. And for now, that is enough for me. Maybe this is what experiencing the Holy Spirit is all about.

XVIII

BOW TO THE DIVINE
WITHIN YOU

Lane tells us to come to a "comfortable, cross-legged position" at the top of our mats.

For the last five minutes, I've been lying on my back with my eyes closed in *savasana*, the yogic "resting pose." It's the last of the series of *asanas*, or poses, that Lane has led me and a dozen other students through for the last ninety minutes on the hardwood floor of the Yoga Loft studio near my house in downtown Manhattan Beach.

Telling us to use a "calm, steady breath" in and out of our nose, Lane has guided us through a fast-paced series of challenging poses such as downward-facing dog . . . warrior one . . . forward fold . . . half-moon . . . warrior two . . . triangle . . . standing splits . . . tree. We hold each one and breathe through the difficulty with a soft gaze forward and level breath, as Lane, our muscular teacher with his surfer-guru style, reminds us that our practice is good training for real life outside the studio for when "shit really goes down." As he instructs us to hold a side-angle stretch with our front leg bent and top arm reaching for the sky, he encourages, "Yoga teaches us how to breathe through life's difficult moments. Keep breathing."

Near the end of the session, just before we lean back into *savasana*, Lane announces, "Let's play with some inversions."

Brooke was the first person to introduce me to yoga in 1998, before we were married and were just dating and living in Santa Monica. Me a newbie reporter for *People* magazine, and she an actress. Over the years of doing a yoga practice (granted, I have never been a consistent practitioner, but I have tried), the one set of poses I have never been able to master, no matter how hard I have tried, are the inversion poses where you basically position your body upside down. They are the bane of my yogic existence and I have come to accept my inability with yogi compassion and self-love. OK, not really. It has bugged me that I can't do them!

When I began yoga, we would go to a studio in downtown Santa Monica for community classes taught by a young teacher in the *ashtanga* (or "power yoga") movement named Bryan Kest. His brand of yoga was an offshoot of *vinyasa* in which you "flow" from one pose to another in an almost balletic fashion. The studio would be packed with fellow twenty-somethings in the young Hollywood crowd—actors, writers, performers, journalists like me—who wanted to center themselves and get a lean body while they were at it. Brooke had been working as a commercial actress and had been attending the classes. I didn't realize it at the time, but those were still the early days of what would become a nationwide "power yoga" movement that brought the ancient practice into the mainstream of physical fitness. Compared to many other pop-culture trends (like, say, lip injections, bell-bottom jeans, and giant sunglasses), the yoga movement has grown by the grass roots, with bandwagon-jumping celebs hopping on the trend. Jen Aniston, Gwyneth Paltrow, Ryan Gosling, and Sting all practice yoga, and Russell Simmons has been so devoted of a yogi that he has launched his own studio, Tantris, along with his own yoga-wear line. Recently, an email came into my work inbox from Russell himself, offering every E! employee free, unlimited yoga classes for a month at his studio in Hollywood. Smart marketing. But in the last few months I have started to take four to five classes a week at Yoga Loft in Manhattan Beach, so I politely declined.

Through my thirties and into my forties, I would pick up the practice off and on (mostly off) at various yoga studios. I have done Bikram "hot" yoga, *vinyasa* flow yoga, hatha yoga, Iyengar yoga, and even a class that combined yoga and Pilates that they, logically, called, "Yogalates." But this was never a spiritual practice. I would do it for a workout, to trim the belly fat and just feel less tight.

Over the last few months, however, I have gravitated back to the simple practice of breathing and moving in the flow-yoga style that I learned twenty years ago. I suppose my meditation practice, focused on only breathing, has made this a logical continuation of my inward search for God. In Sanskrit, the word *yoga* has been translated to mean "to unite, to join, or to connect." And I must say, I am feeling more connected—to my mind, body, and spirit. I feel more whole. As for holy, I think I am feeling more like that too.

As I have gone from once a week to now three to four times a week, I have noticed my body aches less, my stomach is not aching with worry as much, and I realize (what yogis have said for millennia) that yoga can be far more than just physical exercise. In fact, it can be a spiritual one and going to class feels like a form of worship, a chance to nourish the soul. After all, yoga, as conceived by its Indian masters some 2,500 years ago, is just another form of meditation—albeit one that uses physical poses to train your mind to focus on the present. But those pesky inversions have proved elusive.

As Lane guides students through their improvised shoulder stands and headstands, feet dangling around the room, I work up the courage to slide my mat to the wall. I breathe calmly and gaze softly as I kneel facing the wall and place my forearms flat and lower my head so the crown is pressed on the floor. I interlace my fingers, forming a triangle with my arms, inside which my head rests as I walk my feet closer to the wall, rounding my back as I inch my feet forward into the setup pose that is called dolphin. And then, using all the shoulder and core strength I have built up in my yoga poses, I lift up my right leg straight into the air, then my left, and straighten them so that my toes are now reaching to the ceiling. Struggling to maintain my balance on my head, my legs start to fall toward the wall when I feel a set of strong hands grab hold of my shins and level me away from the wall. "I got ya," Lane says. "Press down through your arms and breathe."

I hold my headstand, what yogis call "the king of *asanas*," for another thirty seconds or so, then gently lower my feet back to the mat. I stay down on my stomach in child's pose and rest to let the blood recirculate back into my body. The headstand, or *sirsasana*, is believed to bring a series of benefits to the body, including a calming of the nervous system through a draining of the stress hormones in your adrenal glands, a nourishing of the brain cells, an increase in your sense of focus and clarity, stimulating the heart and digestive systems

by improving the absorption of nutrients, and a strengthen-
ing of the spirit. I wonder, Aren't all these supposed benefits
of the headstand exactly what I have been seeking to find all
along? Is it possible that my search for God and meaning and
purpose and serenity—which has taken me from Bible studies, to Scientology classes, to psychic readings, to Easter with
the Kardashians—ultimately brought me upside down on this
yoga mat, in this tiny studio fifteen miles south of Hollywood?
If this pose—and its benefits of unifying my mind, body, and
spirit—is the consummate manifestation of me being whole, is
this all I need to experience to be one with God?

I stop myself. The intention of my yoga practice is to allow
my brain to be a gray mass of stillness—not a kinetic soup that
is overintellectualizing one of the most spiritually enlightened
moments I have ever experienced. Apparently, the only "still"
I know is that I *still* have a lot to learn about being a yogi.

Breathe.

Lane asks us to sit cross-legged, then he gently tells us to
place our hands in prayer at the center of our chest, take a deep
breath, and on the exhale "om" in a group chant. I do. This
Manhattan Beach studio is far from a monastery, but the sense
of calm and oneness I have is real. Lane tells us, as we sit with
our eyes closed, that yogis believe *"om"* is "the sound of the
universe passing through our bodies."

After the chant, I bow my head and say aloud to Lane and
the rest of the class, "Namaste" (pronounced "nom-ah-stay"),
which in Hindu practice roughly means "I bow to the divine
in you." It's my favorite part of every class, and not just because it's the end and I can now drink some water and rest my
middle-aged bones. I like it because it is a reminder that we

all are blessed with individual, divine souls but are connected in our search for peace and love and bliss. As cheesy as it may seem, it is a reminder that we are all One. And the simple act of stating that with a bow and utterance of "namaste" is in itself a spiritual act of recognizing the divine spirit that resides in all of us.

XIX

THE GURU WEARS
PRADA

Getting close to God through a true knowing heals the fear of death,
confirms the existence of the soul, and gives ultimate meaning to life.
—DEEPAK CHOPRA

Hello," Deepak greets us from his perch on the stage on the first morning of his "Seduction of Spirit" retreat. "Anyone want to share why you are here?"

A woman stands up and an assistant hurries over and hands her a microphone. "It is my fortieth birthday this year and I need a reset," she announces with a cracked voice.

Deepak says nothing. He just nods.

Deepak's assistant walks the mic over to another middle-aged woman who, despite this being July, is wearing a wool hat. "I have cancer and need to change the way I live," she says. "I am tired of living in fear of death. I want to embrace life and learn to live in the moment."

The crowd applauds and several women get up from their

chairs to come and hug the frail Deepak follower. Meanwhile, our guru nods slowly, approvingly, seated before us in a black cotton shirt and baggy jeans and black sneakers.

Then a man, among the only twenty or so here out of more than three hundred participants in the retreat, takes the mike and shares, "I want to rid stress from my life once and for all."

Flanked by several pieces of colorful, geometric mandala paintings on easels, Deepak squints at the crowd of seekers through his rhinestone-bedazzled designer glasses. Holding a microphone with a gentle grip, he reminds us, "These are all perfectly legitimate reasons for being here. But the bigger reason you are here is to find out who you are—to find your true, inner self. Not your mind, body, or ego identity. You have come to know your spirit, and, by that, I mean your true consciousness."

The author of over eighty books, Deepak Chopra has been for decades the New Age guru of choice among a legion of civilians and celebrities alike. Now, Deepak would humbly correct anyone who called him a guru, and remind them that he is just a soul. His humility aside, he is also a renowned medical doctor, teacher, writer, and lecturer on everything from the cosmos to the benefits of alternative medicine. From Oprah Winfrey to Michael Jackson to Jim Carrey to George Harrison to Kim Kardashian to Lady Gaga, Deepak has long catered to celebrities—and not because he necessarily admires them. Rather, the man who has been called the Guru to the Stars has made no secret that he seeks to have 1 billion people meditating worldwide in order to create "a consciousness tipping point." And Deepak has said that he views celebrities, and the influence they can wield, as a powerful instrument to make his vision a reality. To Deepak, Oprah and the like are helping him in his mission to create a shift in awareness and consciousness that he believes can "change the world."

Naturally, Deepak has his share of critics—from scientists who blast his "pseudoscientific" studies on the efficacy of alternative medicine to journalists critical of a spiritual leader who has built a multimillion-dollar soul-seeking empire, to Trump supporters angry that Deepak called the president "emotionally retarded," to conservative Christians who rail against his teachings as "Satanic garbage."

I am neither a scientist nor a conservative Christian nor a Trump defender. I am also not a cynical journalist willing to disregard someone's message because they happen to have been so connective with the masses that people have paid to learn from them. I am just a guy who wants to learn more about this widely popular form of spiritual thought and practice that Deepak began popularizing all the way back when I was in college twenty-five years ago. I want to learn firsthand from the man who more than anyone before him (including Self-Realization Fellowship founder Paramahansa Yogananda) has brought Eastern philosophy and meditation to the masses with his books, online meditation studies, TV appearances, and exclusive retreats like this one. After I learn it straight from the guru's mouth, then I can form my own judgments.

Over the next six days at the Chopra Center at the Omni La Costa Resort & Spa in Carlsbad, California, I will learn that Deepak is fascinated with the scientifically proven benefits of meditation and will many times state that he believes someday there will be empirical evidence to support his theories that "states of being" can be transcended through it.

So as modern physicists strive to prove the much-ballyhooed "Theory of Everything" that explains the origin and function of all matter in the universe, Deepak has his own *spiritual* theory of everything that revolves around every individual practicing his custom-made style of meditation that borrows from Transcendental Meditation. Deepak calls it Primordial Sound Meditation or just PSM.

My desire to learn PSM is the primary reason I paid $2,100 to attend this retreat, along with wanting to acquire more knowledge and spiritual tools that I can use in my daily life that will keep me in touch with my inner self as I continue on my journey of faith. After reading up on Deepak's form of meditation that so many celebs have come to tout, I hoped that PSM could bring me even more benefits than the Zen-style, mindfulness meditation that I already have been doing.

Here's how Chopra.com describes Deepak's unique form of meditation that Oprah Winfrey has been raving about for many years:

> There are many different ways to meditate. At the Chopra Center, we offer instruction in Primordial Sound Meditation, a powerful meditation technique rooted in the Vedic tradition of India. Chopra Center co-founders Deepak Chopra and David Simon have revived this ancient practice of sound meditation and made it available in a format that's easy to learn.
>
> When you learn Primordial Sound Meditation, you will receive a personal mantra. A mantra is a specific sound or vibration—which when repeated silently—helps you to enter deeper levels of awareness. A Sanskrit term that translates as "vehicle of the mind," a mantra truly is a vehicle that takes you into quieter, more peaceful levels of the mind.

The mantra you will receive is the vibration the universe was creating at the time and place of your birth,
and it is calculated following Vedic mathematic formu-
las. When you silently repeat your mantra in meditation,
it creates a vibration that helps you slip into the space
between your thoughts, into the complete silence that is
sometimes referred to as "the gap." Your mind is no longer caught up in its noisy internal chatter and is instead
exposed to its own deepest nature: pure awareness.

Curious, I signed up online for the "Seduction of Spirit" retreat, his signature event that is held twice a year at his Chopra
Center at the La Costa Resort and Spa.

At the retreat, attending alongside other meditators from
forty-one states and twenty-one different countries, I have
so far experienced a personal mantra-gifting ceremony; done
yoga every morning; learned how to practice Primordial
Sound Meditation for over thirty minutes twice a day (several
times crying mid-meditation in an emotional release); sat for
lectures from Deepak on everything from quantum mechanics
to his eponymous "Seven Laws of Spiritual Success"; enjoyed
ayurvedic (a prehistoric Indian diet believed to have healing
powers) meals that have flushed (quite literally) my body of
toxins; and I am now experiencing a Deepak-guided meditation exercise in "regression," where he says he will take us
back to our earliest memories, to reunite us with our lost souls.

"Focus on your mantra," Deepak reminds us from his perch
on the stage in front of the rows of chairs where we sit upright,
relaxed with our hands resting on our lap.

Four days ago when I arrived, the night before Deepak's
Monday-morning session opening remarks, I received my

personal mantra. On that first night's opening lecture, Deepak's longtime right-hand man, a soft-spoken Brit and Julian Assange look-alike named Roger Gabriel, gave us a thirty-thousand-foot view of what lay ahead. Roger explained that in the 1980s he and Deepak were part of the TM organization under Maharishi Mahesh Yogi, "one of the greatest teachers of meditation and spirituality."

Roger and Deepak had a falling-out with the TM people over, among many things, how they viewed the best way to bring meditation to the masses, with Deepak believing it needed to be more easily available to all. So Deepak set out on his own, recruiting his close pal Roger to join him in a way that I imagine Tom Cruise did to Renée Zellweger when Cruise's character quit his sports agency in *Jerry Maguire*. Deepak crafted his own offshoot of TM and called it Primordial Sound Meditation. Roger said that the biggest difference between the two styles is that TM doesn't share how they came up with your mantra, but PSM tells you that your three-word mantra comes from a very specific sound of the universe at the time and place of your birth. "The mantra takes you back home inside yourself," Roger explained. "It is just a tool to take us in that inward direction."

Echoing Deepak, Roger went on to explain how meditation is a way to open up what he called "the gap" between thoughts. The gap is a space where there is only "silence and a field of infinite possibilities. It is where our soul resides."

I sit a few rows back tapping every word he is saying into my iPad as Roger adds, "With regular practice we reconnect with our essential nature and learn to integrate the silence and infinite possibilities into our everyday lives. We learn that we can stay grounded, so we don't float out into emotional chaos when something challenging comes our way. With that state of consciousness, then we can do whatever we want, within reason. The only thing that stops us now is our lack of imagination. Meditation takes us into that gap and allows us to bring that into our lives. Every time we meditate, a little bit more space opens up and we learn how to be in here and now and in the moment. The real you—your soul, your true nature—is in the space between your thoughts."

After Roger's opening remarks, I walk across the palm-lined resort to the world-famous Chopra Center, a white Spanish-style building housing Deepak's office, a bookstore, a wellness spa, and meditation and meeting rooms. I sit in the waiting room with a few other attendees, waiting to be escorted back to a meditation room where we will be given our personal mantra. I close my eyes and focus on my breath in the Zen meditation style I have been taught, wondering how different it will be to meditate to a mantra rather than focusing on the breath.

A man with a shock of silver hair steps into the silent room and introduces himself. "Ken?" he whispers, shaking my hand.

I nod yes.

"I'm David," he says, bowing his head. "Please, follow me."

He escorts me down a hallway to a room at the end. The shades on the window are drawn and the room is lighted only by a few candles. A stick of incense burns on a nearby table along with a traditional Hindu offering of fruit and a flower. I slide off my Birkenstock sandals and place my backpack on the floor. We sit facing each other.

David smiles and looks me in the eyes with an earnestness and formal solemnity that reminds me of when I would go to confession with my priest as a kid.

"Are you ready to receive your personal mantra?" he asks softly.

I reply, "Yes."

David says that he will first recite a Sanskrit chant and then give the mantra to me, which had been calculated from the online form I filled out when I signed up revealing my 11 a.m. birth on April 18, 1970, in Buffalo, New York. He asks me to close my eyes. I do. He begins chanting in Sanskrit, most of which to my L.A. ears sounds like gibberish, though I do recognize some "oms" and "shantis" that pop in and out of the melody. David chants for about a minute in this soothing, rhythmic way. He then stops and tells me to keep my eyes closed. He then says, "I will now chant your mantra." I lean forward and David begins repeatedly chanting, "*Om *** namaha . . . Om *** namaha . . . Om *** namaha.*"[3] David then asks me to chant it along with him to memorize it, and after a few chants, he stops and I continue for about a minute. I feel a wave of deep relaxation and then open my eyes. "Do not share your mantra," David explains. "It is yours. To share it will diminish its power to bring you inward."

"I won't," I promise.

"Very good," David says, placing his hands in prayer. "Namaste."

I press my palms together and reply with a bow, "Namaste."

A few days after receiving my mantra, I am seated amid the sea of attendees in the resort's main ballroom listening to Deepak guide us into a "regression" exercise.

In his Indian accent, still quite prominent even after more

---

[3] In keeping with the principles of the mantra-gifting ceremony, I have omitted the middle word in my personal mantra.

than forty years in the United States, Deepak calmly instructs us to close our eyes and simply breathe and focus on silently repeating our personal mantra.

Within a minute or so, my body feels less rigid and my breathing is slower. I sense my body sinking deeper into the chair with every mantra recitation.

Deepak then instructs us to "picture a screen of your consciousness and see yourself today and recapitulate everything that has happened so far." Within a few seconds of his prompt, I picture waking up and writing in my diary in the hotel room, walking to get coffee as it is still dark, doing a yoga class outside on the lawn by the golf course as the sun is rising, sitting in the ballroom for morning meditation session for a half an hour, having lunch with other attendees out on the hotel terrace.

Deepak then says to become aware of any flashes of memories, not in order but just as they come, of the day each of us left home to come here. I see the images of packing my suitcase, of saying goodbye to the kids, of Brooke mentioning that she liked this "new, calmer Ken" who was about to drive down to San Diego for a spiritual retreat, of me arriving at the resort and feeling nervous about what I had just committed to doing for the next six days.

As I swim in the images, Deepak says to recall a significant event from "the last ten years or so" that was emotionally important in some way—good or bad. I round off to thirteen years ago and think of my son Jackson being born. The image is so vivid of my pale baby son with a big head and big blue eyes, of touching his tiny hand in the delivery room and him squeezing it, cementing a bond that is unbreakably beautiful.

By now, I am in a trancelike state as Deepak says to imagine a time in my teens. My mental picture shows a white banner strung across my house that my mom made, reading CON-GRATULATIONS, KENNY! after I had won a world cup hockey tournament. I smile as I relive the moment as clearly as if it were yesterday.

Deepak asks us to remember when we were under twelve and I see me playing baseball with my brothers on a field near our house. The scene plays out like a movie. I am both viewer and participant. My father is coaching us, laughing and hitting ground balls to all of us. I feel my eyes welling with tears. I miss Dad. I want to reach out and touch him, squeeze his hand like Jackson did to mine in that delivery room.

I am emotionally and physically immersed in the regression exercise. I am not asleep, but also not quite conscious. This is the closest I have ever come to having an out-of-body experience. Perhaps I am in "the gap"; maybe I have found the amorphous space in which the soul resides. I am just being.

Deepak then tells us to think of when we were babies, under two years old. At first, I am having trouble, but I soften my mind's eye and eventually an image of me staring up from my crib at a colorful mobile comes before me. It's joyful, innocent, and simple—much in the way that I have been learning this week is our true, natural state of being, before our ego invades and distracts and our nurture of parents, of culture, of traumas overshadows our nature.

Then, in his soothing drone, Deepak asks for us to see ourselves in the womb. My chest is rising and falling on its own, a soothing force of life, as if the universe is passing through me like my yoga teacher likes to describe the sensation. Every muscle in my body feels relaxed. I am in a fully meditative state when a totally black picture emerges before me. I am floating in water and can only hear the pulse of my heartbeat and primordial squishing sounds amid the fluids of the womb.

Under Deepak's spell, I have lost track of time and space. This exercise could have been going on for ten minutes or an hour—I have no clue.

Fully immersed in the moment, I hear Deepak ask us to regress further and see ourselves in "previous lives." A series of images immediately pop into my head. First, I see me in what looks like the 1800s or maybe early 1900s and I am a pretty woman with big breasts wearing a fancy dress, as if I am high society. I don't look very nice or warm. Then I see me as a peasant in some period of time long ago, like several hundred years ago, draped in drab gray clothing. It seems as if I am begging in the streets of some ancient-type place. Then I see myself as a black woman in Africa; I am topless, with big, floppy breasts.

After some period of time, Deepak invokes us to slowly open our eyes and "come back into the present."

My gaze comes into focus as the lights slowly turn back on in the ballroom. It is the evening of July 13, 2016, and my body is in Carlsbad, California. After seemingly having just traveled back in time, I have never felt more in the present. And I came to this sensation, this awareness, by turning off my thoughts, creating a space in which I could just experience my being. By losing my mind, I connected with my soul.

I have found a way to create space for me, a bigger space of self-awareness and peace than the one I have been able to find with my Headspace apps. I had just transcended my physical self. And in that space, in between the breaths and the thoughts and distractions of my life, I found a tranquility that I've never found praying to Jesus, getting my tarot cards read, studying the Bible, or staring at a sunset. It's a place where my stomach doesn't hurt, my mind isn't consumed with worry, and I don't feel shame or guilt that I am not a good enough father or husband or son or brother or *E! News* correspondent. In this space, I am a soul. And I am perfect.

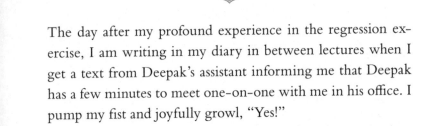

The day after my profound experience in the regression exercise, I am writing in my diary in between lectures when I get a text from Deepak's assistant informing me that Deepak has a few minutes to meet one-on-one with me in his office. I pump my fist and joyfully growl, "Yes!"

I have been trying all week to get some one-on-one time with him through an email off the website, but the *gap* between me and Deepak narrowed after Kelly, a very friendly energy healer on staff at the center, recognized me as "that guy from E!" and put me in direct contact with his assistant, Carolyn.

Shortly before lunch, I walk across the resort grounds to the center, where I am greeted by Carolyn, a kind woman around Deepak's age who has been his personal assistant for decades. She takes me straight into Deepak's office, which is quite small and cramped. Books are strewn across his desk and stacked next to his computer monitor. Framed photos of Deepak with friends, fans, and celebrities litter the office. I know he reminded us in the first group session that he is not a guru, that he is just another soul on a journey, but I am honored he took some time to sit with me.

"Thanks for taking the time to meet with me," I say.

"My pleasure," he says pleasantly. "Here, have a seat."

Knowing I only have five minutes, I quickly tell him how transformational of an experience the Seduction of Spirit retreat has been, especially the regression session.

"What did you see?" Deepak asks.

"I saw me in three previous lives," I reveal. "And they were all women."

His eyes light up. "Oh, that's very interesting now, isn't it?"

"I think so," I say. "How do you explain that? Is that normal?"

Deepak laughs. "Well, obviously, there are no gender constraints when it comes to past lives," he answers. "But it's interesting that everyone you saw was as a woman."

And then it hits me. In my twenties, I was diagnosed with a benign brain tumor that was secreting the hormone prolactin, which women produce to make breast milk. The tumor had depleted my testosterone and over the years feminized my body, until I had it surgically removed in 1998.

I tell Deepak about my gender-bending medical history.

"I was trained as an endocrinologist," he says. "So I am very familiar with these kind of tumors. You had a prolactinoma, correct?"

"Yes," I say. "In fact, a very small part of it is still in my head, and I have to take medication to suppress prolactin production so that the tumor won't grow back."

"Interesting," Deepak muses.

We lock eyes in what has turned into a major "aha" moment for me. And, apparently, for Deepak.

"You know, Deepak," I say, "I've been thinking the whole time I have been here that I am one of only a couple dozen men in a group of three hundred women. And it has really confounded me why men just aren't drawn to spiritual exploration in the same way as women. Now I am starting to think there is something about me that is different, maybe more feminine in nature, and maybe that explains why I am here."

Deepak arches his graying eyebrows and says with a smile, "I think you might be on to something. It's hard to know, or to prove with any scientific certainty, but, anecdotally, you might have some stronger-than-usual connection to your divine feminine."

"Forgive me, but what does that mean?" I ask.

Deepak adjusts his designer glasses as he offers me his Prada-quality explanation. "We all have within us the divine feminine aspect. Some have it more than others. It just depends how far along we are on the path. The notion of the 'divine mother' is of nurturing and of life giving. In Hindu, this is known as *shakti*, which literally means 'divine mother.' She represents power, intuition, compassion, love. These are the highest order of human abilities and it is all feminine—not masculine. Some of the greatest spiritual leaders in history, from Gandhi to Buddha to Jesus, have been depicted as having a feminine aspect in both their conduct and message. And now, in this age of information technology, we are now in a stage where it is no longer survival of the fittest, but rather survival of the wisest."

I purse my lips in thought. "So does the fact that I maybe was a woman in previous lives and my body has a tendency to overproduce a female hormone make me more, I don't know, spiritually evolved?"

"Makes sense doesn't it?" he says with a grin.

Deepak looks at his watch. "Anything else you would like to discuss?" he asks.

"Actually, yes," I say. "Real quick because I know you are busy. I wanted to tell you that I have worked in Hollywood for twenty years, and I have been covering the lives of celebrities very closely. I know you have worked with many celebrities over the years. I am just curious to ask you why you think so many celebrities have so many personal struggles."

"Well . . ." Deepak begins with a breath, his hands folded flat on his desk. "In general, I find celebrities insecure and narcissistic. As someone said, the ultimate selfie-taker was Narcissus. And now technology has made this level of narcissism possible for everyone—and celebrities may be at the top of the list. But at the same time, I think that if they weren't narcissistic and insecure they wouldn't be successful. But the problem is that their insecurity drives them—until they burn out. And inevitably, they do. And that leads to addictions and all kinds of things and problems. They begin to believe in their own press. They take themselves too seriously, and if they don't get the same attention they're used to getting they start feeling insecure and use all these escapes because they literally burn themselves out. So it's a kind of a contradiction and a paradox. The more successful they are, the more insecure they get because they are only as good as their last movie, last show, their last song, and if the next one doesn't do as well, they think they are a failure. It's their whole identity. So, frankly, I feel sorry for them."

"But you've helped a lot of them," I say. "And I am not some huge celebrity or anything, but you've really helped me this week."

He smiles and says, "Really, Ken, I hope that what you

learned here this week is that there is nothing you need help for. You are getting the tools right now, but everything exists inside you. You don't need answers. You just need to live the questions."

On my way out, Carolyn snaps a photo of me with Deepak, my left hand placed over my heart with gratitude.

Later in the day, Deepak is leading the retreat group in our evening meditation. After half an hour of peaceful, silent meditation, Deepak rings a bell, our cue to stop reciting the mantra and to listen to his next instructions.

"Now, ask yourself these soul questions," he says. "And answer them silently to yourself."

"Who am I?"

I am.

"What do I want, what is my deepest desire?"

I want to be.

"What is my dharma, my purpose in this life?"

My dharma is to be a light of love and insight.

"What am I grateful for?"

I am grateful for everything.

⚓

Back up in Los Angeles, after meditating almost daily for several months and dedicating myself to a yoga practice three to four days a week, I am feeling spiritually enriched and emboldened like never before.

It's a Saturday morning. Following my yoga class in Manhattan Beach I drive north up the Pacific Coast Highway to make a pilgrimage. I have been putting this off, busied myself with my newfound yoga, meditation, and a creative writing life that is more inspired and has me feeling liberated, satisfied, and content. But there is someone with whom I still must commune.

Thirty minutes later I arrive in Pacific Palisades. I park my car and stroll into the lush garden and sit alone on a stone bench overlooking a lake on which sit a few swans and lotus plants. I admire the wisps of clouds that look like they're not sure whether to let the late morning sun break through just as my thoughts, my hang-ups, my fears, my existential questions once formed a clouded barrier between me and my spiritual self, between me and the equanimity that comes with finding the divine within me, that comes with knowing God. But after spending the better part of the last year dedicated to my search for God in Hollywood, and exploring with an open heart many different spiritual traditions and practices, I still don't know how to define this more mindfully aware, more present, more peaceful state I have been enjoying and how to label the practices I use to achieve it.

And that is why I am here on this bench amid the tranquility of L.A.'s Lake Shrine Temple, a lush spiritual oasis of palms, statues, and chapels founded in 1950 by Paramahansa Yogananda, one of the first prominent Indian yogis who came to the United States with the goal of introducing Americans to yoga and meditation. Yogananda dubbed his ten-acre meditation garden near the southern end of Malibu "a temple without walls." And it certainly feels like that.

Before settling onto the bench, I had walked down a stone path that rings the tiny lake past a patch of grass on which sits a display called the Court of Religions. It honors the world's five principal religious traditions with symbolic monuments: A cross for Christianity, a Star of David for Judaism, a wheel of the law for Buddhism, a star with a crescent for Islam, and the Sanskrit character for "*om*" for Hinduism. The respectful nod to all major faiths is a symbol of the fundamental respect and tolerance that Yoganada held for all religions. The charismatic yogi believed that we could experience a personal relationship with God through different traditions with the help of meditation.

According to his 1946 book *Autobiography of a Yogi*:

> Central to Paramahansa Yogananda's teachings, which embody a complete philosophy and way of life, are scientific techniques of concentration and meditation that lead to the direct personal experience of God. These yoga methods quiet body and mind, and make it possible to withdraw one's energy and attention from the usual turbulence of thoughts, emotions, and sensory perceptions. In the clarity of that inner stillness, one comes to experience a deepening interior peace and awareness of God's presence.

In my twenty years living in L.A., I must have driven on Sunset Boulevard past this compound perhaps hundreds of times. In fact, when I lived in Santa Monica in the late 1990s my apartment sat only five miles away from this spiritual sanctuary for meditation and prayer. But in my ego-minded focus on the material at the expense of the spiritual, I had always considered myself "too busy" to take even just a few minutes to come and reflect here, even though I had heard about friends doing weekend-long silent retreats in the cabins on the temple grounds and having picnics and enjoying the peace.

The first time I remember hearing about the Lake Shrine Temple, which is operated by the unity faith movement called The Self-Realization Fellowship, was in 2001. Beatles member George Harrison, a longtime practitioner of Transcendental Meditation and a follower of Eastern spiritual beliefs, had just died, and his funeral was held inside the dramatic, white sanctuary that sits atop the cliff above the lake. Harrison so believed in the mission of the Self-Realization Fellowship (SRF) that he donated all proceeds from the reissue of his 1970 song "My Sweet Lord" to SRF.

The temple, I learned, had long been a welcoming place of worship and reflection for the celebrity set—Elvis had famously visited here in his heyday. An archway frames a memorial to Mahatma Gandhi, complete with a vault filled with some of his ashes. Prior to his death, Steve Jobs had planned for every attendee at his memorial service to receive a gift in a brown box: a copy of *Autobiography of a Yogi*—a book that outlined the practice of transcending your individual, physical self through yoga and meditation in order to reclaim your true universal self or soul.

The temple and grounds is as close to a holy site as you can get in Hollywood and, in fact, it is visited by thousands of tourists every year and is believed to be the most visited religious site in Hollywood. And today, after spending the last few weeks taking a break from things like churchgoing, psychic readings, and Bible study, I have instead focused on meditating, doing yoga and, most recently, reading books on Buddhism. All this has led me to come here for some reflection, pondering, and to begin conversing with the ultimate voice.

I close my eyes and my self-dialogue starts with a voice that speaks in the same soothing tone I use during prayer and meditation.

"I don't think I will ever be able to have faith in any single religion," I say.

That is not a failure. The Buddha taught his students not to accept what he was teaching just out of faith in him or what his teachings said. He warned against having blind faith in anything and every-thing. The Buddha actually encouraged his followers to simply listen, investigate, learn, and experience his way. That is how he said one can find absolute, eternal truth and, ultimately, a state of nirvana, enlightenment.

"But I want to have a defined faith and it bothers me that I don't have anything to call it, no matter how hard I try. It's not peaceful for my mind to not have been able to figure it out."

Ah, the mind. It is known to be a terrible cause of suffering, which is why the Buddha teaches that the fundamental state of life is one of suffering. That is, humans experience pain and misery that comes from the conflict caused by trying to attach ourselves to things that are transient and impermanent, by craving to control things that are ul-timately uncontrollable. It is a state of being human, but it is also in your capacity to end this suffering.

"Gee, thanks." I sniff. "So after all my searching for peace and love and happiness, you're telling me that life is suffering? That's not a very optimistic take on life."

When studied closely, you learn that Buddha's teaching is actually infinitely hopeful. If you break it down, you will learn Buddha taught a total of four basic "Noble Truths" of human existence. The first is the truth of suffering. The second is the truth of the cause of suffering, craving things that are not permanent (like money, youth, physical immortality, trying to solve an unsolvable problem, or attachment to material things) . . . the third is that suffering ends with enlightenment, which is attainable by everyone . . . and, fourth, that we can reach this state of nirvana through following what he called "The Middle Way," what he called the "Eightfold Path." So, you see, Buddhism is, on the contrary, very optimistic in its principle that eternal bliss and happiness is available to everyone. The Buddha Nature is one of liberation, of compassion and understanding, positivity, and love.

"Sounds a lot like all the other religions," I muse.

Indeed, it is in many ways, but it is more of a philosophy than a religion in the traditional sense. Perhaps, Ken, that is why you've come here, to a temple that honors all the great religions. The Buddha honored all religions and bowed to their divine.

"So how do I once and for all try to find nirvana?" I ask. "I am forty-six. My mortal life is in the halfway-over range, so I don't have a lot of time to figure this out."

First of all, you have an infinite amount of time. Secondly, you don't need to try to be a Buddhist. In the Zen tradition, they call this state of being "shikantaza," or just sitting. Other traditions call it other things. But it's all about just being still and meditating.

"So it's all about turning off the mind in order to turn on the spirit," I say.

Yes.

"I have been doing that, actually."

Oh, you have? That's great. Then you are on the Eightfold Path!

"Yeah, well, sort of. I mean, I am not a monk or anything. But I've been doing some guided meditations in which I am focusing on the breath and learning to let go of thoughts and feelings as they come in and out. I have been doing mantra meditation every day for, like, twenty minutes a day."

And have you experienced the state of non-thinking, where you aren't focused on an object or a breath or a mantra?

"Yes. I mean, not for a very long time, but maybe for a minute here and there."

Then you definitely have practiced just sitting! The Buddha taught that in this state your mind is empowered to have profound insights into the meaning of life. So, Ken, what has being still taught you?

I stop and think. This is a very big question. Perhaps the biggest of this midlife spiritual quest I have been on.

Finally, I reply, "I have learned that there is an infinite capacity for stillness inside me."

You sound a lot like the Buddha.

"So, does that mean I am a Buddhist?"

It means you are just "being"—there is no need for labels, Ken. The ego mind likes labels, but the inner, true self likes just being. You can be Christian, Jewish, Muslim, Hindu, atheist, and you still can practice just sitting. When you do this, you can feel the light of God.

"So maybe I have found God?"

Buddha didn't use the term "God" or speak of other divine deities. But if by "God" you mean that you have felt peacefully blissful and liberated, even for just brief moments, then, yes, sure, you could say you have experienced the power of God.

"But to be a Christian, the New Testament says that I have to believe that faith in Jesus Christ is the only way to heaven."

Do you believe that?

"No, I don't."

But the Bible, in the Book of Psalms, also says, "Be still, and know that I am God." Sounds familiar, right?

"Yes—and very Buddhist."

There is truth in the Bible. There is truth in the Buddha. Truth is truth, no matter who is speaking it.

"But not all of the Bible speaks truth to me. For example, my heart tells me that Jesus, while a very significant historical figure, is not the one-and-only Messiah. I think it's fine for people to think that and embrace that as their truth, but my heart doesn't."

Trust your instincts. Trust your heart, Ken.

"I also feel as if a lot of the Hindu philosophy I have learned from yoga and from studying with Deepak Chopra and learning about Buddhism makes more sense to me than Christianity. But I wouldn't call myself a Hindu either. Same goes for Islam. I have read the Koran and it's a very loving, redemptive message about how to live and know God, the very same God of the Judeo-Christian tradition, but I am not capable of putting all my faith in Allah and his laws, as is outlined in the Koran. Heck, I even found the psychics who I saw were channeling a spirit world and have a lot to offer me. Now can you see why I can be confused at times?"

The Buddha says that meditation will bring you the answers and all the insight you need to know the truth.

"I *can* believe in that wisdom. But even then, I am learning there are so many different kinds of meditation and prayer practices. How do I know whether TM or PSM or Zen meditation or Christian or Islamic prayers are the way to go?"

Follow your bliss. To the Buddha, if it brings you serenity, mindfulness, and insight, then you are on the right path. Keep observing all your thoughts and feelings, see them for what they are—fleeting moments—and they will no longer control you.

"But what is the best way to meditate? Is it the mantra method I learned from Deepak, or is it better to have my breath be the object of my focus?"

They both have the same purpose, and all methods of meditation can lead you to the same state of mind. For many, a mantra can take you into a deeper state of what has been called absorption. But Anapana-sati—or mindful breathing—is also effective.

"I like to use both."

Then use both. Whatever you choose, just make it a practice and stick to it. No matter what your object of focus is—the breath, a thought, a mantra—as long as it brings you to that state of warm bliss, that is all that matters.

"Well, meditating has definitely made me less stressed, less hostile, less distracted, more, well, just happy. This, I do know is true. But if I call myself a Buddhist or a yogi or a free-agent spiritualist, any label makes me feel like I am closing myself off to other paths that will lead me to the same place."

Ah, yes, feelings, emotions. Remember this: The Buddha identified that people can have 84,000 different emotions.

"Wow, I thought there were like maybe ten—max. You know happy, sad, confused, excited, scared, et cetera."

Humans are complex beings. And remember that feelings come from thoughts. So meditation, when practiced properly, can eliminate thoughts by learning to let go of them. While meditating, you focus on your breath, and when a thought or feeling breaks that focus you say, "OK, there it is," without judgment, and then you focus back on your breath. And to the Buddha, that freeing of thought, then of feeling, will bring us to a state of detachment from our physical reality, which will then bring you liberation. Ultimately, it will bring the end to suffering.

"So I only have to eliminate 84,000 emotions from my body and I can reach nirvana?"

Basically, yeah.

"But I'm afraid I have some bad karma built up from Hollywood."

We all have it. Our actions, thoughts, and words can harm people. The Law of Karma states that there are inescapable results of our actions.

"Exactly my dilemma! I go on TV and online every day and, well, I often talk shit about famous people. On any given day, I might criticize a reality star with enormous lip injections for looking like a clown, or cast judgment on a pop star for flubbing their lyrics, or I might say one of many other true yet harmful things about someone. I worry that I can't fulfill my job requirements while also being loving, peaceful, and mindfully aware."

It's only bad karma if it is motivated by greed, hatred, or delusion.

"Greed." I sigh. "I say all these things for my job because, frankly, E! pays me to utter them, to spew judgmental words that can harm people. So am I doomed?"

Do you, in the course of doing your job, report or say things that are motivated by generosity, compassion, or wisdom?

"Honestly, yeah. I will always say if someone is really talented, or beautiful or they did a great job and stuff like that. I will applaud celebrities when they say or do things that I think are admirable. I'm not a total bad karma machine."

Well, that is good! These all are deeds that bring wholesome or "good" karma. The Buddha taught that we can endeavor to practice morality and compassion in all that we do, and that will bring about as much good karma as possible. The Buddha said that we reap what we sow.

I ponder his karmic wisdom, and wonder whether I can ever dig myself out from under the twenty years of bad karma accumulation as a Hollywood journalist by focusing on creating good karma and moving forward. As daunting as it may seem, I am willing to try. Hey, if I can't overcome my karma in this life, perhaps I can in a future life after I experience what Buddhists call rebirth, and Hindus call reincarnation. If there is such a thing, of course. Or, then again, maybe I am doomed after all.

"I just don't know," I say, my dejection dripping from my voice like sweat on an Oscars red carpet. "I fear I might have to stop doing this Hollywood thing. If I stay at E! and keep reporting on celebrities it seems like I am just accumulating bad karma. It's like the spiritual equivalent of running five miles only to get home and eat five cheeseburgers and a plate of fries. It's spiritually counterproductive. Ugh."

I think you will find this a challenge in most any part of modern American life, Ken.

"But Hollywood is probably one of the hardest places to live the way of the Buddha. I mean, it is based on so many things that are antithetical to his teachings—it's an industry obsessed with bodies, youth, beauty, wealth, gossip, and ego. And I get paid to focus a spotlight on all of it. If I stay working in Hollywood, it would be like a recovering alcoholic working at a tequila factory. I am starting to believe there are too many distractions from living mindfully."

Then what would you do? Bear in mind, no matter what you do to make money and support yourself and your family, to stay on the path to enlightenment, you must follow the Eightfold Noble Path:

1. *Right Understanding*
2. *Right Thought*
3. *Right Speech*
4. *Right Action*
5. *Right Livelihood*
6. *Right Effort*
7. *Right Mindfulness*
8. *Right Concentration*

"Tell me more about three and five—Speech and Livelihood," I say. "Those seem to be major trouble spots for me as a Hollywood journalist."

Let me break them down for you: To practice Right Speech is to refrain from telling lies, slandering others, saying things that can bring harm to people, or engaging in foolish gossip.

"Well, then I wouldn't be able to call Justin Bieber 'Justin Boober' anymore."

Probably not. The Buddha taught that you can speak your truth, and offer opinions, but that you must use words that are friendly and benevolent. And if you can't, you are to practice what he called "noble silence."

"This is a huge problem. Whenever I fail to take a position or offer a provocative point of view on whatever news of the day, my bosses make me feel like I am not doing my job. In other words, at *E! News* if I were to practice this so-called noble silence—which is like my mom's old adage of 'If you don't have anything nice to say then say nothing at all'—I would eventually get fired."

Karma, indeed.

"Exactly. I would then have no livelihood."

Well, the Buddha taught that a Right Livelihood is one in which you have a job that doesn't intentionally bring harm to others. Can you do your job at E! News *and not harm others?*

"I don't know."

Well, have you tried?

"No, but I can try. Or maybe I will just write books and just teach writing and help people find their voice, share their truth with the world. Or maybe I should sell my house and open a yoga and meditation studio. I don't know. My paycheck from *E! News* makes my kids' lives a lot more comfortable, pays for them do things that give them a better life."

Are you sure they need your money to have a better life? You grew up in a family that, at times, didn't have much money at all.

I have no answer.

But in this moment I am OK with not having an answer to what the future holds, and, actually, I find peace with not knowing. It makes me feel human.

Instead of racking my brain as I have spent nearly all my adult life doing, I sit on the bench and practice "noble silence." And I keep meditating, taking several minutes to just breathe in and out. A thought about being hungry and wondering what I will eat for lunch breaks my focus. But I don't grow anxious or upset. I don't beat myself up for not being a good meditator. I don't get so distracted that I take myself out of the present and into a mental game of gymnastics that keeps me from enjoying . . . well, just being. As I have been taught, I acknowledge my thoughts, and then gently go back to the breath. Slow and steady. And within a couple breaths, I forget I am hungry and I am at ease and inside. It's taken me several months of daily, solitary practice of sitting, but finally it hits me: I haven't just been practicing how to meditate; I've been practicing how to live.

I bow and mouth a silent "*Namaste.*" When I open my eyes

and look beside me, the space on the bench is empty. I glance around the secluded patch of grass by the lake and no one is there either. Doesn't matter. The voice may not be visible, but he is fully present within me. When I get up and step out of the meditation garden, I feel closer than ever to finding God, closer to myself. I am not stricken with self-doubt. I do not feel alone. I am not lost. I am certain I am walking on the right path.

By the time I pull out of the temple's parking lot and glide down the hill toward the ocean, the morning haze has lifted and the sky is clear. I drive along the Pacific Coast Highway headed for home. The sun's reflection is glaring off the ocean to my right, and I can see that the water of Santa Monica Bay is calm, level, serene. Over the past year, I have been able to enjoy momentary glimpses of such placid equanimity in my life. Today, my soul feels nurtured and my entire being feels mindfully aware of the present, each moment, the here and now that is the miracle of life. I am filled with gratitude.

When I began my spiritual journey I was a man who could barely get through a single anxiety-laden day without popping a Xanax, couldn't get on a plane without having a panic attack, couldn't ponder my mortality without growing depressed or worried, couldn't accept or give love fully because I didn't adequately love myself. But now, though far from perfect or enlightened, I am a transformed man. I am empowered with a mindfulness that dwells within, and I know I can access it by simply closing my eyes and taking myself inside to that space between the thoughts, between the emotions, between the distractions of my media-saturated Hollywood life. In this sacred space, I have found more than peace. I have found myself.

My spiritual journey has taken place almost entirely in and around Hollywood, the very place where I had lost touch with my faith.

The heart of Tinseltown lies a few miles ahead of me as I cruise east down the 10 Freeway with no pains in my stomach, no busy thoughts of worry and concern and overthinking about yesterday or tomorrow. I glance down at the symbols of hope, faith, and love tattooed on my left forearm. They are no longer just an inked cross, anchor, and heart. They are not just symbols. They are what I am.

I roll down the freeway filled with a peaceful, easy feeling, staring out before me at everything and nothing at the same time. I take in a breath, then let it out with a smile as bright as the California sky.

XX

BE

Be.

Revelation

I am driving my kids to hockey practice. Bonding with them in the car like this, just talking about life and enjoying the scenery, has served as my happy parenting place from the time they were old enough to talk.

My son, Jackson, now thirteen, lounges in the backseat of the SUV watching YouTube videos on his phone; my daughter, Chloe, sits in the passenger's seat, so smart and wise and mature and curious for a twelve-year-old.

I am steering through the drought-dry coastal California hills, and when we reach the crest and begin rolling down the western slope toward the ocean, I point out the blue sky that is dotted with a white puff of clouds as if on a canvas before us.

"Look, Chloe," I say. "It's like God painted that."

"Do you believe in God, Dad?" Chloe asks.

"Yes, absolutely," I reply.

"But what kind of god?" Chloe follows. "Like, do you mean nature, or like the Bible God? Or like Buddhism stuff?"

I am taken aback, for I had never had an answer explaining my faith to my kids—until now. I nod and say, "I believe that there is a God, a force, a unifying spirit or energy. But I believe that different religions are all ways to get closer to and relate to the same God."

"What about Jesus?" Chloe asks. "Do you believe in him?"

"Well, I don't **not** believe in Jesus," I explain "I think he really existed and he taught us many things and it's very possible it's true. So I guess I believe in him as much as I can without having met him and interviewed him myself. But I am still trying to figure it all out. There is more study for me to do."

"So what religion are you?" Chloe asks.

"As long as it doesn't hurt people, as long as it is about love," I reply, "I am OK with any religion that brings you closer to your concept of God."

As Chloe lets my answer sink in, I add, "You know how there are all these different languages people speak? Like there's English, French, Italian, Chinese, Japanese, German—hundreds of them. They all exist in order for us to communicate and relate to each other. I think religions are that way too. Christianity, Buddhism, Hinduism, Judaism, Islam, yoga, meditating, whatever the practice, whatever the belief. They all hold great value and can bring us closer to God. They are just different languages speaking to the same God."

"So you definitely believe in God?" Chloe asks.

I pull over to the side of the highway and put the car in park. I look in the rearview mirror as Jackson pulls his gaze from his phone and I can see his blue eyes reflecting back at me. I turn and focus my big brown eyes on Chloe's big brown eyes. Then, gazing back out through the windshield, all I see is the universe staring back at me.

"Guys," I finally say. "I believe God is everywhere."

ACKNOWLEDGMENTS

I am grateful for my family who love me no matter how far I go off the deep end.

I am grateful for all the spiritual mentors, teachers, and co-seekers who appear in this book for trusting me, sharing their stories, and opening up their hearts.

I am grateful for my agents, Jane Dystel, Michael Bourret, and Miriam Goderich, who have always guided and nurtured my writing career. I am grateful for the entire team at Convergent Books who thought God was a worthy search topic—even in Hollywood.

I am grateful for the friends, far too many to name here, who always listen to me, help me, lift me, and believe in me (and pick up the phone when I call on my long, lonely L.A. commutes).

I am grateful for the readers who have invested their time, energy, and attention to join me on my spiritual journey as they travel on their own.

I am grateful for *everything* that has happened in my life—including the perceived good and bad—for they all have been great teachers.

I am grateful for every breath, the sound and sensation of God that gifts this endlessly fascinating, challenging, inspiring, and awesome experience that is life.

THE KEN COMMANDMENTS

⚓ CELEBRITY INDEX ⚓

THE KEN COMMANDMENTS

⚓ SUGGESTED READING LIST ⚓

10 Mindful Minutes, Goldie Hawn with Wendy Holden (Perigee, 2011)

The 15-Minute Prayer Solution, Gary Jansen (Loyola Press, 2015)

The Alchemist, Paulo Coelho (HarperOne, 1988)

The Art of Happiness, The Dalai Lama (Riverhead, 1998)

Autobiography of a Yogi, Paramahansa Yogananda (Self-Realization Fellowship, 1946)

Become a Better You, Joel Osteen (Howard Books, 2007)

A Beginner's Guide to Meditation, edited by Rod Meade Sperry (Shambhala, 2014)

Buddhism Plain and Simple: The Practice of Being Aware Right Now, Every Day, Steve Hagan (Broadway, 1997)

Conversations with God (Book 1), Neale Donald Walsch (Putnam, 1995)

Dianetics, L. Ron Hubbard (Bridge Publications, 1950)

Going Clear, Lawrence Wright (Knopf, 2013)

The Great Eight: How to Be Happy (even when you have every reason to be miserable), Scott Hamilton and Ken Baker (Thomas Nelson, 2009)

The Happiness Project, Gretchen Rubin (Harper, 2009)

The Holy Bible, New International Version, (Zondervan, 1973)

How to Know God, Deepak Chopra (Three Rivers Press, 2000)

Jesus Is ____, Judah Smith (Thomas Nelson, 2013)

A Life Worth Breathing, Max Strom (Skyhorse, 2010)

Loving What Is, Byron Katie (Harmony, 2002)

Manual of Zen Buddhism, D. T. Suzuki (Grove Press, 1960)

The Power of Intention, Dr. Wayne W. Dyer (Hay House, 2004)

The Power of Now, Eckhart Tolle (New World Library, 1997)

The Return of the Prodigal Son, Henri J. M. Nouwen (Doubleday, 1992)

The Seven Spiritual Laws of Success, Deepak Chopra (Amber-Allen/New World, 1994)

There's No App for Happiness, Max Strom (Skyhorse, 2013)

Tuesdays with Morrie, Mitch Albom (Broadway, 1997)

The Untethered Soul, Michael Singer (New Harbinger, 2007)

Way of the Peaceful Warrior, Dan Millman (H. J. Kramer, 1980)

When Things Fall Apart, Pema Chodron (Shambhala, 1997)

The Yoga Bible, Christina Brown (Godsfield Press, 2003)

Zen and the Art of Motorcycle Maintenance, Robert M. Pirsig (HarperCollins, 1974)

Zen in the Art of Archery, Eugen Herrigel (Pantheon, 1953)